Mason Hughes—named "Good M. New Guinea in recognition of his years of service and love for them—has written this compelling story of divine intervention. Poignant and powerful, the book draws the reader to new levels of faith and hope as accounts of God's miraculous reach are demonstrated through the transforming work of the gospel in this nation. Arrows—once symbols of war—became symbols of peace to the tribes through the redemptive power of God! Take hold of this book and receive a fresh understanding of a profound heritage as told by a missionary after God's own heart!

—Dr. Glenn Burris Jr.
President, The Foursquare Church

The title was probably all you needed to pick up this book, but the title only hints at all God did in Papua New Guinea through the ministry and leadership of Mason and Virgene Hughes. And while this book is about God's supernatural power in the past, it also holds forth the expectation that God still moves in power through His people today. As you read about and rejoice over the miracles and changed lives, ask yourself, "Why not here and now?" and then, "Why not me?" The Holy Spirit is filling the church to overflowing, and He will fill you for His great exploits through you!

—Dr. James C. Scott Jr.
Director, Foursquare Missions International

From the tribes of Papua New Guinea to the high-rise executive buildings in Singapore, with simplicity and compassion Doc and Virgene have made a mark on humanity. As their pastor and long-time friend, I have been privileged to hear their stories and humbled to be a part of their lives. Answering the call of God to go into all the world, they have seen the power of Jesus bring salvation to savages, deliverance to the demonized, healing to the hurting, and even life to the dead! This book, *5,000 Arrows*, is the true story of a couple whose sole desire is to let their light shine before men so that the world can see their good works and glorify their Father in heaven (Matt. 5:16). May the Hughes' miraculous journey of faith serve not only as a testimony of what God has done through them, but an inspiration of how He can use you to change your world through the power of Jesus Christ!

—Dale Jenkins
Lead Pastor, New Hope Worship Center,
Concord, NC

Dr. Mason Hughes is one of America's premier missionaries. He is courageous, strong, and humble. His blend of intelligence and grace has made him a mighty warrior in the kingdom for many years. The people of Papua New Guinea and the world have been mightily blessed because of the life of Mason Hughes. Thousands have come to Christ and many more will come to Christ because of the sacrifices he and his family have made. I am so proud to say I am a friend of Mason Hughes.

—Ricky Temple
Pastor, Overcoming by Faith Ministry,
Savannah, GA

5000ARROWS

Dr. Mason + Virgene Hughes Jr.

Rom. 10:13-14

5000 ARROWS

MASON & VIRGENE
HUGHES

HAROLD & DENISE
ABNER

CREATION
HOUSE

5,000 Arrows: A True Account of Christ's Supernatural Power among Cannibals and Headhunters by Dr. Mason and Virgene Hughes and Dr. Harold and Denise Abner
Published by Creation House
A Charisma Media Company
600 Rinehart Road
Lake Mary, Florida 32746
www.charismamedia.com

This book or parts thereof may not be reproduced in any form, stored in a retrieval system, or transmitted in any form by any means—electronic, mechanical, photocopy, recording, or otherwise—without prior written permission of the publisher, except as provided by United States of America copyright law.

Unless otherwise noted, all Scripture quotations are from the New King James Version of the Bible. Copyright © 1979, 1980, 1982 by Thomas Nelson, Inc., publishers. Used by permission.

Scripture quotations marked KJV are from the King James Version of the Bible.

Scripture quotations marked NIV are from the Holy Bible, New International Version. Copyright © 1973, 1978, 1984, 2010, 2011, International Bible Society. Used by permission.

Scripture quotations marked NLT are from the Holy Bible, New Living Translation, copyright © 1996. Used by permission of Tyndale House Publishers, Inc., Wheaton, IL 60189. All rights reserved.

All stories are original as told by Mason and Virgene Hughes.

Some stories revised from *5,000 Arrows* transcribed and authored by Sidney Moore, 1973 by C.F.M. Press, Pico River, CA. Used by permission.

All photos provided by the Hughes family collection.

Design Director: Bill Johnson
Cover design by Marcos Huasta and Nathan Morgan

Copyright © 2014 by Mason Hughes
All rights reserved.

Visit the author's website: www.5000arrows.com.

Library of Congress Cataloging-in-Publication Data: 2014937542

International Standard Book Number: 978-1-62136-753-6
E-book International Standard Book Number: 978-1-62136-754-3

While the author has made every effort to provide accurate telephone numbers and Internet addresses at the time of publication, neither the publisher nor the author assumes any responsibility for errors or for changes that occur after publication.

First edition

13 14 15 16 17 — 987654321
Printed in Canada

We dedicate this book to our Lord Jesus Christ, who is and will always be the author and finisher of our faith (Heb. 2:12). We are humbled by His many blessings and callings on our lives and the opportunities He has provided to serve Him.

We also dedicate this book to the leadership of The Foursquare Church, as they were willing to entrust us and support us to go into all the world and share His gospel.

Thirdly, we dedicate this book to the people of Papua New Guinea who responded and received the gospel of our Lord Jesus Christ, which brought supernatural transformation in their lives.

And lastly, this book is dedicated to our loving family. They persevered and stood by us through all the good times and difficult times for all the years that we served on the foreign mission field—especially our five children: Stephanie, who married Larry and works with him in the county store they own in Bladensburg, Ohio; Bruce, who married Kay, served four years in the USMC, and retired after twenty-eight years in the Ohio police force; Sondra, who married Gordon who retired after thirty-four years working at the Freightliner plant in North Carolina; Michele, who married Bob who builds car engines for NASCAR; and Denise, who married Hal who retired from the U.S. Army and both serve in their local church.

Thank you. We love you all.

Hughes family, 2014 (left to right—back row: Denise, Michele, Sondra, Bruce, and Stephanie; front row: Virgene and Mason)

CONTENTS

FOREWORD

HAVING BEEN RAISED in a warm and inviting, solidly evangelical home from infancy, I had the benefit of an exposure to missionary stories as a part of my Christian education. How well I remember references made by pastors in sermons and by my teachers in Sunday school, as they related unforgettable accounts of the lives and ministries of such historic pioneer missionaries as William Carey (India, 1793–1834), Hudson Taylor (China, 1855–1900), and Adoniram Judson (Burma, 1813–1850).

These men, with their devoted wives, penetrated these spiritually darkened nations in an era when the "cost of surrender" to mission service required the loss of all domestic comfort, communication, and certainty of cultural acceptance or physical security, transferring to locales with little if any medical care available. They were among the earliest of modern "heroes of the faith" who carried the torch of the gospel into seemingly hopeless circumstance. It was such as these, who early matched the fame of presidents, warriors, and sports heroes in the mind of young Jack Hayford prior to and during my teenage years.

It was near the close of those years, in answer to the call of God on my own life, I entered LIFE Bible College in Los Angeles where I began my studies toward becoming a pastor. Little did I know that virtually simultaneous with my mid-term entry in January 1952, I would cross paths with a senior student named Mason Hughes, who was nearing graduation in June of that same year. And little did I know that man would become one whom, with his wife, I would consider entirely worthy of having their names placed beside those missionary pioneers of nearly 200 years earlier. As you read, you'll understand why; and, quite possibly, I can well imagine your concluding the same as I have. So, step into these pages and read of a Stone Age people who stepped from spiritual darkness into the transforming light of Jesus Christ.

This book is the amazing story of God's hand reaching into the miry darkness of South Pacific jungles, touching the blinded, oft-tormented souls of primitive savages; bearers of weapon—arrows being foremost as they wage war against one another. Bound in the grip of superstition and demonically inspired traditions, hope of resolving this self-ruin would take more than education, sociology, or religion to transform people. To bring order and meaning to life for an entire people group, it would take the power of God's love, brought by a man of relentless passion to reach otherwise "throwaway souls" at the expense of all comforts and at the risk of his life.

This is the story of Mason Hughes—and one that equally evidences the heroism of his wife Virgene, who not only shared an equal commitment to Mason's mission but who bore and raised children in the highlands of Papua New Guinea where this remarkable couple served for twenty-three years.

I feel an unusual sense of honor to be invited to introduce this history-making pair and to invite you into their story. I do so, beginning with my words above, to express a respect for the Hughes that is shared by thousands of others who know them; fellow pastors and leaders in the Foursquare Church movement.

This global-mission-minded and affiliated fellowship based in the United States is of Pentecostal tradition. However, we share in common a generous commitment to a full-hearted, interdenominational spirit—one upheld by us all. To be "Foursquare" is to readily and consistently indicate our respect for all traditions that seek to spread the message of God's Word and the testimony of His Son Jesus Christ—the Light of the World and the Savior of mankind. This is the gospel message—and it is the conviction of that host of faith-ignited people who go to the ends of the earth; from the center of troubled inner cities in America to the vine-tangled pathways of central Africa or the diseased masses on the banks of the Ganges in India. They are compelled within to do so—to go with a motivation inspired by God's love; a mission that not only brings the truth of Christ's life, light, and transforming power to those they serve but that the byproduct inevitably brings with it a transformed society still reflective of its uniqueness as people but no longer without the blessings God's way engender in the practical values bring health, hygiene, education, and self-respect.

To conclude, let me confess: I was tempted to ask Mason if I could include the first story I ever heard about him; one related by another friend who early had followed the Hughes's to learn of their mission. But I haven't asked, because the story is his to tell; and here, it is yours to read. (But you can get a head-start by imagining yourself wading for miles, waist-deep through a leech-infested swamp.)

There is drama here, there is warfare—both tribal and spiritual; but the most moving are the outcomes that, for example, were wonderfully evident in so many ways I witnessed myself in 2006 when I was privileged to speak at the fiftieth anniversary of the Foursquare movement in Papua New Guinea. There, among the slopes of the Highlands, I saw multiplied thousands gathered in festive garb, jubilant with joyous song, exuberant in vibrant worship, and united as one with celebrative feasting—their beaming, black, and beautiful faces shining a radiance begotten of divine love, assembled from nearly 1,000 churches which dot the map from the coastal cities to the yet-unsettled regions of the Highlands.

However, ultimately it is the permanently transforming nature of what God's grace achieves over time. The proof of the power of the truth of Christ and the gospel in action exceeds the delight of a single celebration. There, I was visibly moved to tears to participate and to witness that event; but my emotion was stirred because the event was actually ignited fifty years before—the present tally of thousands began with Mason and Virgene's faith, obedience, and sacrifice and with the first handful of people who experienced the grace of God and the power of the Truth that frees individuals, then households, then tribal fiefdoms bringing divine order, hope, and peace where it would otherwise be yet unknown.

Among the delights in reading *5,000 Arrows*, then, is that it combines an adventure with a lasting reality; demonstrating what happens when the "real deal," when God's gift to mankind in sending His Son to redeem us is ministered by "real deal" servants of His, the *fullest* outcome is realized. It is then and there—be it New York City or Papua New Guinea—*the joy, health, peace, sanity, and wholeness found when God's intention for human beings finds it practical, functional, spiritually transforming fulfillment!*

Such an outcome transcends political stability, social reform, religious tradition, or educational enlightenment. It achieves the objective of the full power of the gospel—to shatter the bonds of superstition, break the arrows of human hate, and overflow individuals with the spirit of peace, power of pure love, and fulfillment of the potential development of a fruitful and practical domestic and community life.

There is nothing more adventurous that seeing *this* objective realized in any culture—in a home, a neighborhood, a city of high rises, or a jungle village.

Begin your read. The adventure story here is true!

—Dr. Jack W. Hayford, Chancellor
The Kings University
Dallas and Los Angeles

ACKNOWLEDGMENTS

WE WANT TO give a great big thank you to our son-in-law Hal and daughter Denise. It was their inspiration and prodding to write all the wonderful things God did through the people of PNG that made this book possible. Hal transcribed every word from a recording we used to tell the stories, and Denise did much of the research to help verify anything that needed clarity. Thank you, Hal and Denise, from the bottom of our hearts. We love you.

We first met Steve and Diana Richardson and their family when they pastored in Michigan and we had services with them when we came on furlough. We have always loved them dearly. Now they have come along side us to help us write our book, and we have come to love them even more. The most difficult part of writing a book, we find, is how to find words to say thank you to such lovely, precious people as Steve and Diana. From the bottom of our hearts, we want to thank you, Diana, for editing our book. We appreciate your great wisdom in helping us find the right words to say and your precious spirit in which you so kindly and patiently changed all our add-ons and corrections to the stories. You have displayed a true spirit of love and dedication to the Lord with your talents and your willing heart to see it done well. May your reward for your untiring labor on this book be souls added to the kingdom of God as they read the contents of it. God bless you.

PREFACE

One generation shall praise Your works to another, And shall declare Your mighty acts. I will meditate on the glorious splendor of Your majesty, And on Your wondrous works.
—PSALM 155:4–5

TO PUT INTO writing the many experiences of our family's life in the primitive country of New Guinea, today known as Papua New Guinea, would be virtually impossible. The particular circumstances surrounding the various happenings created spiritual and emotional feelings which cannot be put into words. The purpose of this book is not to give a day-by-day description of our lives as missionaries. We have recorded some of the experiences that were exceptional and have attempted to paint a picture that gives a glimpse of the conditions, culture, and customs of the Highland people of New Guinea where we ministered. Considering there were at least 750 indigenous languages and estimates of over 1,000 different tribes found throughout the island of Papua New Guinea, what is written in this book would not apply to the whole country but primarily to the people in the area of the Eastern Highlands where we ministered. Sometimes just over the next mountain or around the next bend in the trail there are different customs and languages and even different styles of dress.

Papua New Guinea is one of the most rapidly developing countries in the world; it took its place as an independent nation in 1975. Because of this, many of the customs we saw and experienced these many years ago are either extinct or near extinct today. Christian missions have played a large role in the development of Papua New Guinea, along with the government. There is still a close relationship between the two, especially in the fields of health and education. As the first prime minister of Papua New Guinea, Michael Somare, has strongly encouraged the people of his country to develop independence. In the New Guinea Foursquare Church, we attempted to do the same thing. We purposed to establish a totally indigenous work, one that is self-governing, self-supporting, and self-propagating. And that happened! PNG Foursquare is now entirely led by national leaders and they are even sending out their own missionaries to spread the gospel to aboriginal tribes in Australia and in the islands of the Pacific. In a telephone conversation I had on April 11, 2014, with Southeast Asia Missions Director Jerry Stott, the current membership of the Foursquare church in PNG is approximately 85,000, with 1,700 churches and meeting places led by 2,000 pastors. There are orphanages, Bible colleges, and several institutes training leaders. We can only step back, look with awe, and praise the Lord for the mighty acts He has done!

The title of the book is reflective of the arrows I gathered over the years—arrows that had been hand-crafted to take human life. How did I accumulate those 5,000 arrows? I began by receiving them as trade goods for items such as soap, matches, and salt. I also received them for services such as treatment at the medical clinic. The natives had no money but they always wanted to give something back. I bought some from them so they could have money to buy other goods they wanted. Collecting the arrows became a sort of hobby, interesting curios to bring to the States when we were on furlough. But as the warriors received the

Prince of Peace, tribal wars ceased and the men began to bring me their man-killing arrows as a token of their acceptance of a new way of life. These men "went no more out to war." For centuries the arrows had been their symbols of strength and war, but now the men wished to part with their man-killing arrows because the transforming power of God had changed them into Christian brothers. These arrows took on new meaning as symbols of peace, symbols of hearts that were changed, symbols of a new beginning for the people of Papua New Guinea.

When there is no moon in New Guinea, the nights are so dark that it is impossible to see at all. The spiritual darkness that engulfed the land before we came was just as dense. But Jesus, "the light of the world" (John 8:12), changed that. Today "the people who walked in darkness Have seen a great light; Those who dwelt in the land of the shadow of death, Upon them a light has shined" (Isa. 9:2).

The stories that make up *5,000 Arrows* are of the people who were the beginning of the New Guinea Foursquare church, how they found Christ, and how they are growing in Him. This story covers some of the years of my life as a missionary in that land. It is thrilling to reflect on the good things God did during these years.

—Dr. Mason Hughes
Ordained Foursquare Minister and Missionary

Chapter 1
LIFE, COURTSHIP, AND MARRIAGE

Therefore a man shall leave his father and mother and be joined to his wife, and they shall become one flesh.
—GENESIS 1:24

I N A WAY of introducing ourselves, we wish to give you a brief look at who we are, how we met and married, our training and calling, and the early days of our ministry.

Mason

I was born January 6, 1929. I was raised by my parents, Mason and Pearl, in a Christian home along with my two sisters, Edith and Lorraine, and brother, Clyde. We attended a Baptist church because we lived in the country and did not have a car and that was the only one near our home. My dad worked for the Southern Railroad as a telegraph operator. I dropped out of school after I finished the eleventh grade. My first job at sixteen years of age was in Danville, Kentucky, on the fire department. When I was seventeen, my sister Edith invited me to come to Dayton, Ohio, to live with her and get a job. I moved to Dayton and got a job at National Cash Register. Edith took me to church with her to Christian Tabernacle. I had strayed from the Lord; but I rededicated my life to Jesus during a Luther Mieir revival. I would go to church every time the doors opened. I thoroughly enjoyed the praise and worship part of the services. It seemed like the Lord ministered His love to me while praising His name during the song service, especially those stalwart hymns of days gone by, such as "I'll Go Where You Want Me to Go." One song in particular rings through my mind even today, "Speak, My Lord" written by George Bennard in 1911:

> I hear the Lord of harvest sweetly calling,
> "Who will go and work for Me today?
> Who will bring to Me the lost and dying?
> Who will point them to the narrow way?"

> Speak, my Lord, speak, my Lord,
> Speak, and I'll be quick to answer thee;
> Speak, my Lord, speak, my Lord,
> Speak, and I will answer, "Lord send me."

There were many other songs that spoke to my heart. I would go to almost every service, sit in the front of the church, and end up kneeling at the altar to offer myself to His service.

Virgene

I was born November 18, 1929. I have one brother, Harold Albert, ten years older than I. We were raised in a Christian home and attended a Pentecostal Foursquare church called Christian Tabernacle. My parents, Evan and Mildred Price, were active in the church. My daddy was nearly always on the church council and was also head usher. Mother was head hostess, which was quite a job as it was a church of 800. Daddy worked at the Frigidaire plant for twenty-five years. One night when I was sixteen years of age, all of us girls noticed a very handsome young man who had begun coming to the church. We sat in the youth choir on Sunday night so we could all see who was in the congregation. It ended up that three of us were really drawn to him, but we thought he was already married as he always sat with a young lady. He was very much a gentleman; he would help her on and off with her coat and sit with his arm around her during church. Then we found out that she was his sister! So the other two girls each invited him to go somewhere with them. One was the pastor's daughter and the other was the Sunday school superintendant's daughter. I just went home and prayed about him. He was really handsome and had a neat gold front tooth.

Mason

As I sat in church next to my sister, Edith, I noticed a beautiful little lady on the front row of the youth choir on Sunday nights—she had a beautiful smile. I found out her name, Virgene Price. After awhile I was able to meet her and I found out who her parents were. That scared me! But one night I asked if I could walk her home from church, as she and her parents lived just a couple of blocks from the church. It was on my way home as my sister lived a couple of blocks farther. So she said yes, I could walk her home. That was in March of 1946. Things began to grow with our friendship.

Virgene

My first real date with Mason was when I was a senior at Parker Co-op High School. Our choral group was going on our school bus to see an opera. So I invited Mason to go. He wasn't sure about an opera, but he was happy to be with me. We had a neat time. I graduated from high school in August of 1946, and Mason was there. Then our church had a revival. The speaker was from the Assembly of God church. He was very drawn to Mason. They spent a lot of time together during his short stay. My parents had also become very fond of Mason. Of course, our relationship was growing very steady; and yes, we were falling in love.

It was a bit confusing for me, as this was my first real relationship. When I was thirteen years old, one time I was praying at the church altar and Jesus very plainly said to me that I was going to marry a minister. I hid this in my heart and did not tell anyone—even my parents. Then one day Mason said to me, "What would you think if I went to Bible college?" My heart leaped with joy, and I said, "I think it would be wonderful!" That was in October of 1946. In November he proposed to me. Of course, I did not have to think twice before I said, "Yes!" Then there was the deal of telling my parents. Since my brother Harold had married when I was only eight, I had been their only child. My mother was not sure about giving me up. So things and plans began to grow. I received my diamond for Christmas.

Mason

The love between Virgene and me was growing stronger and sweeter. But I also knew that God had called me into the ministry. Virgene had shared with me her calling to be a minister's wife. The Assembly of God minister that I had become acquainted with suggested that I go to an Assembly of God college in Waxahachie, Texas. Of course, that meant Virgene and I would be separated. We talked about it and knew that God was planning our future. We just had to be still and wait for Him to show us. So in January 1947, I took a Greyhound bus bound for Waxahachie, Texas. We did not have the money for phone calls, but we were very faithful in writing letters almost daily. I got a job at the fire department to pay for my schooling. I could also stay there at the fire department, so that took care of my lodging. After starting college, I was able to pass an exam that gave me my high school diploma. I enjoyed the school time, but I really missed my special gal! By spring we were so longing to see each other that I hitchhiked from Texas to Ohio. I surprised Virgene by meeting her when she was walking home from work. I hoped that she would not faint! We enjoyed being together for a few short days while I stayed with Edith. Then I took the bus back to Texas. When the semester was over, I came back to Dayton.

Virgene

By then I knew that I, too, wanted to attend Bible college like Mason. But I wanted to attend LIFE in Los Angeles, the Foursquare Bible college. So we discussed our future. My father still loved Mason very much, but by that time my mother had turned against him somewhat. She could not face the idea that I would leave home and she would have to give me up. Mother and I had become very close through the years. But I knew that Mason was the one God had chosen for me; and as the Bible says, I wanted to leave my parents and cleave to my husband. He wasn't my husband yet, but he would soon be. So along with my plans to go to Los Angeles, my Father took three months off from his job so they could take me there. Then, he said, they would go on down to San Diego and live. Mother would not let Mason ride in the car with us. He had to take the bus. So he arrived in Los Angeles ahead of us.

Mason

Wanting to be near to Virgene's college, I was planning to transfer my credits to the Assembly of God school in Pasadena. I had arrived early so I had some time before school started. I wanted to see what Virgene's school looked like, so I got on a city bus and found LIFE Bible College. I was walking by Angeles Temple (the mother church for Foursquare), when I met Dr. Charles Hollis, the pastor at that time. We had met him previously at a Sunday school conference in Moline, Illinois. God has His own ways; praise the Lord! So Dr. Hollis asked me, "What are you going to be doing for the next few days?" Labor Day was coming up. I said "Nothing." He said, "Why don't you go with me to Camp Cedar Crest for a retreat." So off we went. After Dr. Hollis found out a bit of our story, He told me, "You don't need to transfer to Pasadena. Why don't you just enroll in LIFE?" So when Virgene arrived, we shared the glorious news.

I soon found a room with several other male students. Virgene already had her room in the girl's dorm. But her parents did not keep their promise of moving to San Diego. They found a little house to rent right between Virgene's dorm and the school so her mother could keep an eye on her. Yes, what fun! We had only been in school a few weeks when we made an appointment with Dean Teaford to tell him our story and ask if he would marry us. The school policy was that you had to be in school for three semesters before you could get married. But we were already engaged, so that made a difference. When Dr. Teaford heard our story, he said, "I'll tell you what I will do. Give your mother one semester to see if she will change her mind. If she does not, I will go ahead and marry you." We were a bit disappointed, but we agreed. The legal age for a boy to marry without parental permission was twenty-one. But there was no problem getting permission from my parents; they had fallen in love with Virgene. The legal age for a girl to marry was eighteen, and Virgene turned eighteen in November.

Virgene

Mason and I soon made a lot of friends. Among them were Aubrey Hurt and Irene Ghere. Irene became my roommate. After Mason and Aubrey would drop us off at the dorm—we had a 10:30 p.m. curfew, they would take off in Aubrey's old Ford and

6

paint the town red. Soon our semester was up. At least we were able to enjoy sitting together; this was allowed since we were engaged. Mason had a job at a high-class department store downtown as a stock man in men's clothing. I was working at a bank as a bookkeeper. Between us we barely made enough to pay our tuition and board.

As the semester came to a finish, we went in to see Dr. Teaford again. He told us that we could be married in the fourth floor school auditorium at no cost, and that he would dismiss all the classes so the students could come to our wedding! Wow! So we began to make plans. We bought matching Glenn Plaid suits. I choose green shoes, and Mason got a green bow tie. We had enough money to buy plain gold wedding bands. We chose two of our friends to stand up with us. I carried a small white Bible with baby orchids on it and streams hanging from it.

Mason

For Virgene and me to get married, we knew that we would have to get a marriage license. But in the midst of wedding plans, I had spent all my money—so what should I do? I had a lovely black-faced watch that I had bought for $150 while working at National Cash Register. So I took it to a pawn shop and got $5.00 for it—enough to get our license. When I got to school that night, Virgene said, "Where is your watch?" I had to tell her; of course, she had a fit. She had enough money left for the license, so she made me go back and get the watch the next day. One more thing; I had been laid off from my job three weeks before our wedding date. But we decided to go ahead and get married since Virgene was still working and they had promised to call me back to work. And they did call me back—while I was getting dressed for the wedding! It was my boss; he asked, "Can you come to work tomorrow?" I responded, "Oh, I'm getting married tonight." He said, "Okay, come in the day after." Great!

In making the plans for our wedding on February 9, 1949, we had asked Audrey Mieir to play. She was a well-known song writer and had her own youth choir. Virgene had known her since she was six years old. She was happy to play for our wedding. Virgene's father knew about the wedding and wanted to come so badly, but he could not. He had given Virgene's mother sleeping tablets hoping she would not disturb the service. Also, Dr. Teaford did not want anything to disrupt our wedding, so he had put Temple guards at each of the many doors, just in case Virgene's mother arrived. Yes, it was quite a time! He talked about our wedding for years later.

We met in Dr. Teaford's office. He went out first to the platform, and our attendants followed. Then Virgene and I walked out together. We paused at the bottom of the steps, and Virgene sang the song "I Love You Truly" to me. We went on up on the platform and had the ceremony. The auditorium was full—some 250 students. We did not have a car, so our photographer (a classmate) took us to our hotel at the beach for our one night and day honeymoon. We walked the beach and had a great time eating huge shrimp. Our classmate came and got us and brought us back.

Virgene

Where did Mason and I go when we came back? It was during the Korean War, and it was really hard to find a place to rent. We found an Italian family who were renting their one-car garage. We washed the dishes in the bathroom sink, we had a two-burner stove to cook on, we rented a fridge to use, we had a bed to sleep on, and we were close enough to walk to school.

That was enough; our needs were met. We didn't care—we were in love.

When we asked our photographer about our wedding pictures, he was so sad to tell us that he had forgotten to put film in the camera. Fortunately, Mason had given me a little Ansco camera for Christmas and we had given it to someone to take pictures for us. To this day, that is *all* we have; but that's better than nothing.

A couple of days after the wedding my parents packed up and went back to Dayton, Ohio. My mother just could not accept the fact that she was not losing a daughter but gaining a wonderful son-in-law. We found out later that my brother and sister-in-law had the same problem; but she did attend their wedding where I was the flower girl. Yes, my mother finally accepted Mason after I became pregnant with our first child, Stephanie, who was born in 1951.

Mason

We graduated from LIFE Bible College in February of 1952 and were assigned to pastor a small church in Durham, Canada. Our son, Bruce, was born in 1953. A couple of years later we were notified that the annual Foursquare conference was to be held in Decatur, Illinois. There were two lady Foursquare pastors living near us at the time. They said they would love to attend the conference and would pay for gas if we would drive our car. That worked out great, except that Bruce became ill on the Sunday prior to our planned road trip. This was not so great! The lady that was going to babysit Stephanie and Bruce for us while we were gone encouraged us to go ahead. She offered to look after both of them and see them through. Virgene, pregnant with our third child, protested right away stating that she would not leave

9

her sick son. She desperately wanted me to go ahead. She resolved to stay and look after the children and sent me on my way.

So the two other pastors and I ventured out to the conference with an attitude of expectation and anticipation. One night at the conference they sang the refrain, "I'll go where you want me to go, dear Lord." This same song had ministered to me during numerous song services in the past, but never like what I was feeling that night. I went forward, knelt at the altar, and prayed like never before. Right after I prayed, I heard Dr. Harold Chalfant, the guest speaker for that night, boldly pronounce, "If you really mean business with the Lord, I have an application for you to fill out to become a missionary!" All these years I knew I had a calling on my life. This statement struck a chord in me. I immediately answered in the affirmative and shouted, "Yes, Lord! 'Here am I! Send me'" (Isa. 6:8).

So, I went up to the platform, took the missionary application, and filled it out completely right then and there. I knew, without a doubt in my heart, that this was Virgene's desire as well. My emotions were running wild! I felt exultation and yet I felt at peace. I also had a gnawing doubt that maybe nothing would happen. But, I knew that I obeyed my heart and that the next step was the Lord's to take. Although I didn't play any kind of musical instrument nor had I taken a single missions class at Bible college (I had pursued the pastoral track for my degree), I trusted God to direct my path and left it at that.

When I arrived back home after convention, I quickly greeted Virgene. I was so excited to tell her how the Holy Spirit had prompted me while at convention! I asked her, "Guess what I said yes to while I was at convention?" She responded, "Knowing you, it could have been anything!" When I told her what I had done, she was extremely happy. Both of us felt a bit nervous as to the magnitude of my actions, but we left it all in the hands of the Lord.

Five months later I went to the post office. We did not have mailboxes at our houses back then. I was surprised to find a letter from the Foursquare Missions Department in Los Angeles. I could hardly wait to get home and open the letter with Virgene. I ran into the house and called Virgene to the kitchen table. I excitedly told her we had a letter from the Foursquare Missions Department to open together. We soon discovered that this letter announced to us that we had been accepted to be Foursquare missionaries! We both nearly fainted!

After collecting ourselves, we continued to read and reread the letter. The letter asked us one key question: "Where do you want to go?" That was a piercing question, for we had no place in mind. We had no specific calling to any people. We both knew we were meant to go. But where? We both fell silent. We knew one thing for sure. We desired to take the name of Jesus some-where—somewhere where people had never heard of Jesus before.

After very little discussion and in total agreement with each other, I excitedly wrote back and explained to the missions board that I had no specific place in mind. I had no country preference. I had no feelings one way or the other. I knew, though, that I was to go where there were no missionaries. I knew that I was to go where the people had not heard before. I knew that God had impressed upon both our hearts Romans 10:8–15:

> But what does it say? "The word is near you, in your mouth and in your heart" (that is, the word of faith which we preach): that if you confess with your mouth the Lord Jesus and believe in your heart that God has raised Him from the dead, you will be saved. For with the heart one believes unto righteousness, and with the mouth confession is made

unto salvation. For the Scripture says, "Whoever believes on Him will not be put to shame." For there is no distinction between Jew and Greek, for the same Lord over all is rich to all who call upon Him. For "whoever calls on the name of the Lord shall be saved." How then shall they call on Him in whom they have not believed? And how shall they believe in Him of whom they have not heard? And how shall they hear without a preacher? And how shall they preach unless they are sent? As it is written: "How beautiful are the feet of those who preach the gospel of peace, Who bring glad tidings of good things!"

Our missions department quickly responded, letting us know that they wanted to open some new countries for Foursquare missions. One of those new countries was New Guinea. That sounded great to both of us. But first we had to find it on the map; we had no idea where it was! Not even anyone from our missions office had ever been there!

By this time Sondra Jane had arrived. We were encouraged to move back home to Dayton, Ohio, to be with our families while we made preparations to go. We filled out so many medical records, applications, forms, and papers. We applied for visas. We applied for passports. The missions office did not want to take any chances, so they had us get every immunization they could think of. We set about preparing ourselves for a journey halfway around the world to a people that we had never seen, who spoke a language that we had not learned, in a country that we had just found on the map!

The missions department was able to arrange space for our family of five as passengers on a Swedish cargo ship with six other passengers. This was another new experience. None of us had ever been on a boat or a ship or even a canoe on the water. I grew up on a farm; solid ground and dirt were our things. Anyway, after boarding the ship and sailing rough seas for twenty-three days, we docked in Sydney, Australia. We were met by some lovely pastors who took care of us until we were able to arrange a flight to the capital city of Port Moresby, New Guinea.

And that's a little bit of history about our life, courtship, and marriage before we began the work in New Guinea.

Chapter 2
OFF TO THE DARK BEYOND

Leave your native country, your relatives, and your
father's family, and go to the land that I will show you.
—GENESIS 12:1, NLT

HERE WE WERE at 9 p.m. on a July 1956 night gathered at the Dayton, Ohio, train depot and surrounded by family and friends. Mason was holding nearly three-year-old Bruce Mason, who could care less as he was sleeping on Daddy's shoulder. Five-year-old Stephanie Marie was holding on to Virgene's dress, not sure of what was really happening, while Sondra Jane, eight months old, was sleeping in Mommy's arms.

Mason's parents, Mason and Pearl, were there, along with his sister Edith and family, our pastors Rev. and Mrs. Roy and Blanch Lewis, and many other church friends. Why were we all there? We were about to embark upon the next phase of our ministry. We were saying good-bye to our family and loved ones for five long years.

On February 19, nearly six months before, the missionary application which Mason had filled out to go to New Guinea was accepted by the Foursquare Mission Board. We were pastoring in Durham, Ontario, Canada, but moved back to Dayton to prepare for our adventure. We had diligently checked all the large libraries nearby to learn all we could about New Guinea, but we could find no information—only a picture of the beautiful bird of paradise.

At the time we were accepted to be missionaries, Foursquare did not know any more than we did about New Guinea as no one had yet visited that country. So they wanted us to get every immunization possible before we left. One day when we went to the doctor's office, we could not find Bruce. He knew what was coming and was hiding under a table in the back corner. Poor little guy, he had had enough shots. Within a couple of days, he came down with the mumps. When we contacted the doctor, he informed us that because we had taken so many injections so quickly, little Bruce's resistance was down. In just a matter of a few days, Stephanie also came down with them. We felt so bad for them. By the time we got on the train, they were no longer contagious. But, since Stephanie was still a bit swollen, Virgene made two big ribbon bows and put them on the little yellow bonnet she wore so no one would notice.

Now that the preparations and arrangements had been made for our new adventure, we were ready to say good-bye to our family and friends and board the train that would take us to Los Angeles. From there we would go on to New Guinea, that new, strange land that would be our home—a country about which we knew nothing.

After boarding the train we found ourselves in the coach car for our three-day journey. We were young and excited, so this seemed merely an insignificant inconvenience to us. In due time we arrived in Los Angeles, happy to be back at LIFE Bible College, our home for our college years until we graduated in February of 1952.

We were met by our wonderful mission director, Dr. Herman Mitzner. He was appalled to find that we had been sitting up in the coach car with our three small children for the previous three nights. Checking with his office staff, he found that there should have been arrangements made for us to have a berth for sleeping quarters on the train. Our experience just made us all the more appreciative of the wonderful bed we slept in that night. Dr. Mitzner felt so badly about the whole incident that he took us shopping the next day and bought each of us a wonderful outfit of clothes. God was looking out for us!

Meanwhile, God had been looking ahead in another way. We needed a letter to present to the government of New Guinea, a guarantee of accommodations, before they would give us a visa to come into the country. God helped us solve this problem through Ron and Margaret Teale, who had been missionaries in New Guinea with another organization. After they had received the baptism of the Holy Spirit, they had been released from that organization. They went on furlough in Sydney, New South Wales, Australia, where they found the Foursquare church in the suburb of Greenacre. About that same time a young man from that area, Don Baker, felt a call to go to Bible college and enrolled at LIFE in Los Angeles. Don Baker connected us with the Teals. By the time we were ready to go to New Guinea, the Teals and their two daughters, Esther and Ruth, had returned to New Guinea and were employed at secular jobs in Port Moresby, the port of entry. We were able to get our letter of accommodations through them.

Not everything was rosy, though. On the second morning after we arrived in Los Angeles, Virgene woke up with swollen jaws. The mumps wanted to make another appearance. Mason phoned the missions office, two blocks away. Immediately Dr. Mitzner, a man of faith, came and prayed for her and the swelling went down. Thank Jesus for His healing power!

The missions office had made a booking for our family to sail on a Swedish cargo ship, the *Parakula*, on July 25. There would be eleven passengers, and we would be five of them. The exciting day finally arrived!

CROSSING THE PACIFIC

Dr. Mitzner took us to the ship. Our hearts were beating very fast—first of all because we were leaving our country and family for such a long time, but mainly because we were heading for a land that we knew nothing about. We had no idea what the country looked like, what the people looked like, what any of their customs were, or whether they knew anything about Jesus. But we knew one thing: our lives were dedicated to Jesus to minister wherever He could use us, even on the mission field.

Mitzner with Hughes family ready to board the ship

We boarded the ship and found our state rooms—yes, rooms! Mason was in one room with Bruce, and Virgene was in the next one with the two girls. There was a crib for Sondra, which was a blessing. When mealtime came, much to our surprise we dined with the staff, the captain, and his officers. What wonderful food! While pastoring our small church in Canada, we had lived on $10 a week to take care of the family. God always supplied all our needs and we never went without, but the captain's fare was luxury indeed! On a cargo ship there wasn't much for the children to do, and we had to watch them carefully as the decks were not always safe. We did enjoy the water, and seeing the ocean with all its majesty was so wonderful!

On the fifth day of sailing, Mason woke up with a swelling at his neck. We cried out, "Oh, Jesus, this can't be!" We prayed just as Dr. Mitzner had done for Virgene, but Mason's swelling did not go away. Even in the midst of trial, God again was looking ahead for us. As we reported Mason's condition to the captain, he remembered that a hostess they had hired for the dining room was an RN. She was tired of nursing and wanted a break so had signed on the *Parakula*. Isn't God good! She began to look after Mason. By the second day the fever had gone up to 105 degrees and Mason was very sick. He was actually delirious for most of several days. Virgene stayed with him as much as she could when others looked after the children.

We sailed for twenty-three straight days and saw land only once—Fanning Island. That was a refreshing sight. By that time Mason was not contagious and could sit in the lounge. We spent many hours discussing what kind of missionaries we would be. We agreed that we would be "spiritual" missionaries; we would focus on the spiritual needs of the people. We would just preach the gospel. We thought it best not to be encumbered by being concerned with medical, teaching, agricultural, or other "physical" needs they might have.

We were nearing the end of our voyage. Before we were allowed to dock in Sydney, a doctor had to come on board to make certain that Mason was no longer contagious. The captain was happy to hear when the doctor gave the "all clear" so that the ship could dock. What caught our eyes as we looked at Sydney were the roofs on the houses—all red tile and so pretty.

Australia

We were all glad to have our feet on solid ground again. As we got off the ship, there were several there to meet us: Pastor Banton, Stan Baker (Don's father), Pastor Mortimore, and others. A chilly breeze met us also. No one had told us that the seasons were opposite on the other side of the world, so it was winter in Australia. We knew that we were going to the tropics, so we had brought only light clothing. As we were transported to our new accommodations, we realized that we were driving on the opposite side of the road. Wow! That was a bit scary! In those days the homes in Australia did not have central heat, so to help with the cold they got us a little kerosene heater to use. They were also kind and found us some warm sweaters, coats, and blankets. During the month we were in Sydney, we spent a lot of hours in bed—just to keep warm!

During the day we would take walks. On our first day we passed a chemist (drugstore) with a weighing machine out in front. We wanted to check our weight, as we knew we had gained weight with all the rich food on the ship. We looked at the machine, and it said to insert one pence. "What is one pence?" we wondered. We went inside and asked the man at the counter. He knew by our accents that we were foreigners. He gave us a handful of large coins, which he told us were each a pence. So we put one in the machine and out came a card that told us our weight in stones! "What is a stone?" we wondered. We went back in the store. The man at the counter laughed and told us, "Oh, one stone is fourteen pound." So went our education in Australia.

An American missionary couple, Wayne and Dorothy McIntosh, were in charge of the Foursquare Bible college there. After a few days we moved in with them. It was good to have some Yankee friends. They wanted us to share with the students at the college. That was a joy! There we met a young couple, Albert and Nell Booth, with their three children, Eileen, Gordon, and Mark. It was also their desire to go to New Guinea, so we enjoyed talking with them. Later they joined us there.

One afternoon we had a phone call from the Bakers inviting us to come to "tea." Mrs. Baker told Virgene just how to get to their home—this train, that bus, etc. Virgene said to her, "Just a minute. Could you tell my husband how to get there, so we will both know?" Mrs. Baker went through it all again. When Mason hung up, Virgene said, "Do you know how to get there?" He said, "No, I didn't understand a word she said." Virgene commented, "I didn't either." We had not yet learned how to understand the broad accent of some of the people.

So, Dorothy, bless her, got on the phone and got the directions for us. We were to arrive for tea at 7 p.m., so we had our evening meal before we left, as our kids were hungry. When we arrived at the Bakers, wonderful food smells met us. We had not yet learned that "tea" is their evening meal and that they eat late. So we got the children aside and told them, "Just sit down and eat. Don't tell them that we have already eaten." Fortunately, they were obedient. We enjoyed their "tea" of a delicious meal of lamb with all the trimmings. What a wonderful family! We had several times of great fellowship with them. Bruce had his third birthday at their house on August 19, 1956.

The McIntosh's wanted us to stay and help teach in the Bible college, but we knew that God had called us to take His Word to New Guinea. So we made bookings and boarded a DC-9 for the six-hour flight to New Guinea. The children's eyes were very big when we got on the plane, but they were good.

Land of the Dark Beyond

As the plane circled Port Moresby, we saw dry, brown mountains and a dirt airstrip. Our hearts were beating very fast as we realized that this was "our land." When the plane came to a halt, we looked out the window to see a brown-skinned, bare-foot, no-shirt man wearing only a wrap-around skirt as he pushed the steps up to the plane. Words cannot describe the wonderful, overwhelming feeling we had as we said, "Lord, these are the people that You have sent us to minister to."

The plane door opened and a hot September blast came against us; it reminded us of what it must have been like for the three Hebrew men facing the fiery furnace (Dan. 3:23)—it was *so hot*! As we walked to the small terminal, we were met by Ron Teale, our New Guinea contact, dressed in white shorts, a white shirt, and knee-high white socks. We learned quickly that was the proper dress for expatriates (Caucasians) in New Guinea. We were greeted with a big smile and warm Christian love. He loaded our cases in his Land Rover and we drove to their home, just a short distance away. There we met Margaret, six-year-old Esther, and five-year-old Ruth. Margaret had taken on the task of training young men how to be house help by cooking, cleaning, etc. Most everyone had one or two young New Guinea men working in this capacity.

We were shown our accommodation—their enclosed back porch with mosquito nets covering mattresses on the floor. Our children were very glad to have playmates and soon found a tub of water in which they all played. New Guinea is the second largest island in the world, so it has beaches everywhere along the coast. Fortunately, we were only a five-minute walk to the ocean beach, where we spent a lot of time since it was so hot—in the 90s day and night.

We began to pray and seek God, "Where do You want us to go?" We did not feel we should stay in Port Moresby, as there were several churches there already. We felt the Lord would have us to go towards the Highlands; New Guinea is 60 percent mountains. Mason needed to explore and spy out the land, so he booked a flight, as there are no roads connecting Port Moresby to the Highlands.

He flew first to the small town of Wau, which is 3,500 feet above sea level. It was a gold mining town with banks, two very small grocery stores, a post office, and a few other amenities. It was a beautiful little town suited to grow vegetables, which they shipped all over the island. A vegetable farmer had an empty house, so Mason made arrangements to rent it. This was not an easy task, as the companies that employ expatriate people build houses only for their employees.

Then Mason felt he should take another flight on to the town of Goroka, which is 5,300 feet above sea level. When he arrived in Goroka, he met a missionary from New Tribes Missions who invited him out to their station, some two hours away. This gave Mason an idea of what the terrain of the land, the people, and their surroundings looked like—so much more primitive than Wau. The people lived in bamboo huts with grass roofs and wore very little clothing. The clothes they had were made from bark. Mason learned from the missionaries that New Guinea was only 3 percent literate and that in order to communicate we needed to learn a language called New Guinea Pidgin, or Pidgin. Even to use this we would need an interpreter, as there were somewhere near 750 different languages in New Guinea.

When Mason returned to Port Moresby, the family was very excited to find out that we had a house of our own to call home. Soon we said our good-byes to Ron, Margaret, Esther, and Ruth;

thanked them for being so wonderful and hospitable to us; and boarded a DC-3 heading to Wau. It was so beautiful and green at 3,500 feet altitude, quite a contrast from the dry, brown town of Moresby. It was like a cup scooped out of the mountains. The airstrip was just grass with a 350 foot drop from top to bottom because of all the mountains surrounding it.

Mason had arranged for a truck to meet us and take us to our first New Guinea home. It had two bedrooms, a living room, and a kitchen. The windows had no glass but were merely openings covered with screen, what the Australians call fly wire. This helped to keep the mosquitoes out, thank goodness! Because the windows were merely screen-covered, when it rained we had to move all the furniture to the center of the room. One of the fun things about our house was that it was located with a full view of the airstrip; we could watch every plane come in and out. During landing the planes had to use full throttle to land to get to the top of the hill. Then they again had to use full throttle on takeoff or else the pilot would have coffee branches in his landing gear!

Chapter 3

WAU AND BUCKINGHAM PALACE

I will instruct you and teach you in the way you
should go; I will guide you with My eye.
—PSALM 32:8

NEW THINGS EVERY DAY

As we adjusted to life in Wau, we could not find a vehicle to buy, so we soon learned to walk slowly and cautiously on gravel roads. Fortunately we brought Sondra's metal stroller from the U.S., so we could put her in her stroller when we needed to go shopping. The little grocery store was about a twenty minute walk, but in the hot tropical sun it seemed like an hour and twenty minutes. We had to learn how to ask for Australian food. Shortening was lard, Jello was jelly, biscuits were scones, candy was lollies, etc.

By this time we were working on the language. We hired a young man named Kumbu who knew New Guinea Pidgin. He did not know English, so we would perform an action or hold up an item and then write down what we thought he said. This went on for several weeks. As soon as Mason was able to write enough words for a message, he got permission to have Sunday services at the gold mining compound. He would read his messages until he became fluent enough to speak them. Virgene and the children were attending an Anglican church that had been started for the expatriate people. Virgene was teaching Sunday school there. So began our work for the Lord. On November 8 of that year, Sondra had her first birthday with a big cake; and ten days later Virgene had her twenty-seventh birthday.

While we lived in Wau, we had the joy of welcoming the Booth family to New Guinea. They also rented a place there.

They, too, were very excited about telling these primitive people about Jesus. They had three children, twelve-year-old Eileen, nine-year-old Gordon, and seven-year-old Mark. Like most kids, they attracted other kids in the neighborhood and they all had a wonderful time playing. But it wasn't long before Albert felt he wanted to move on. So they went to another part of New Guinea called Sepik Province to the small town of Angoram. We had prayer with them and sadly said good-bye.

After eight long months of walking on gravel roads in the tropical sun, Mason made his usual trip to the post office to see if we had any mail from home. It took three weeks or so for a letter to arrive. He always checked the board at the post office where someone who wanted to sell something could put up a notice. This special day he came home very excited. "Guess what? There is a notice on the board that a lady is going back to Australia and wants to sell her Jeep!" he exclaimed. This was music to our ears! The Mission Board had given us money to buy furniture, but nothing for a vehicle; so we decided to borrow the money from our furniture fund. Shortly Mason bought the vehicle and came home proudly driving our "new" little black Jeep. It was a leftover from World War II, complete with bullet holes. But it worked and had wheels.

Each week Mr. Schrevaner, our landlord, would bring us a box of fresh vegetables. One day he asked us, "My dog has just had puppies; would you let your children have one?" Who could say no? So Sammy joined our family, a little black combination Blue Heeler and Kelpie. We all loved him. Later on we were given a cat that we named Judy.

Never a dull moment! Our Jeep was parked up a small hill in back of our house under a shelter. One day three-year-old Bruce thought he would have a little sit in the driver's seat. The next thing he knew, he had kicked the vehicle out of gear. It coasted down the hill and stopped with the nose of the Jeep right in the kids' bedroom! It knocked the house right off the foundation. Bruce decided he would not sit in the Jeep again—good idea!

Eighteen-day trek

As Mason got more acquainted with the country, he planned a walking trip (a trek) from Wau to the coast going through Garaina. He hired men to walk with him and carry his cargo, as he had to take food and supplies for himself and his carriers. He had to change carriers when the language would change. The foliage and challenges were different with the several biomes they traversed from the high mountains to the coastland and back.

During the walk, he wore shorts and high-top boots. They walked above the ground on the top of tree roots through the jungle where the area was infested with leaches. Every fifteen minutes Mason would stop and scrape the leaches off his legs. One night he found he had missed one leach, and it had buried itself into his leg. By the next night it had become infected; he had a red streak going up his leg and a fever. He lay down on his mat with his boots as a pillow. As he was trying to go to sleep, he heard a commotion. Mason asked the interpreter what was going on. He was told that another white man was coming, a government medical officer making his rounds. He gave Mason some antibiotics and wrapped his sore. Again God was looking after us!

Mason stayed down for a day. He then continued the journey out to the coast and back to Wau. He had been gone for eighteen days with no contact. Yes, there were no cell phones in those days! We knew Jesus was on the throne taking care us; we had no choice but to trust Him. It was a wonderful sight when we saw each other, Virgene driving the little black Jeep out to meet him. She and the children had made many trips out, hoping to see him coming down the road that led into Wau. The eighteen-day journey was arduous, but it confirmed to us that this was not the area to which the Lord was leading us. Today there are many Foursquare churches in and around Wau in the area where Mason trekked.

THIS IS THE PLACE!

Mason felt he should drive the Jeep up farther into the Highlands to search out the land there. There was an Australian patrol post at Henganofi, 5,550 feet up in the mountains, about thirty-five miles from Goroka. In those years the territories of Papua and New Guinea were Australian protectorates. (Later the territories were merged and then given independence as Papua New Guinea—PNG.) Ross Johnson was the Australian patrol officer. Mason found his office and introduced himself. He told him of our intentions to tell the people about Jesus.

Ross was very encouraging. He warmly invited Mason, "Come in and spend the night with us. Tomorrow I am going on patrol to two valleys, the Kamantina and the Dunantina. You can have a look and see what you think. There are no missions in either valley." Mason's heart jumped with excitement! He spent a lot of time in prayer asking God to lead and direct him.

They started out the next day. As they went down the Kamantina Valley, Mason sensed nothing extraordinary. But, as soon as they turned down the dirt road into the Dunantina, the Lord clearly spoke, "This is the place." Ross pulled into a spot where he was going to settle some disputes. It was near a small bush house that Ross said he used occasionally when on patrol. Mason got out and looked across the road at a beautiful piece of property. Again he heard the Lord speak, "This is where I want you to start a mission station." He felt like Elizabeth must have felt when the babe leaped in her womb (Luke 1:41). What joy came over his soul!

Mason turned to Ross and pointed across the road, "Is that piece of land available?" Ross responded, "I think so. But before we can ask the government if you could lease it, we have to ask the people who own it if they want you to have it." The owner was right there. When Ross asked the owner the question, he replied, "Oh, for sure! We would love to have a white man live there." Ross agreed that Mason and the family could live in the bush house until a government lease could be obtained for the land. He gave him permission to enlarge it to make it suitable for our needs.

Ross went back to his station at Henganofi and began the work on getting the lease for the land. To acquire the five acres for the mission station, there were government procedures to go through. First of all, the people had to want us there. This was not a problem. Also, it was necessary for the government to take a census to see if by ninety-nine years (the length of a mission lease) those five acres would be needed by the people. In addition, the request had to go in the *Government Gazette* paper and not be contested by anyone. All of this took time. But Mason knew this was God's holy ground, and it was to belong to the Foursquare Gospel Mission.

Ross held a local meeting concerning the land. Among the several hundred men attending that meeting, there were two men who knew the New Guinea Pidgin language we had been learning. The rest only spoke their native languages. This miracle concerning these two men goes back two years before—at the same time Mason was in America signing the application with Foursquare Missions to come to New Guinea. It was at that time these two men, Kiabe and Tubabufa, had gone to the coast to work. During the two years they spent there, they learned New Guinea Pidgin, the language used widely on the coast. The Lord's timing is perfect.

Jeep adventure

Mason could hardly wait to get back to Virgene and the family—a twelve-hour drive on a one-lane, dirt mountain road—to give them the wonderful news. He had found the place they were to build the mission station and a house for the family! As he drove back down the dirt road to Wau, he had to ford many rivers. If there had been a big rain, he would have to sit in the Jeep and wait for the water to go down. Otherwise he would walk through the river and find the shallowest path across. Then he would find several men, tie a rope on the Jeep, and have them pull it across to the other side. While crossing the Leron River, Mason sat in the driver's seat while the men went ahead pulling the rope. Suddenly the men stopped. One man wanted to go one way and the other wanted to go another way. With the water flowing swiftly, the Jeep began to undermine and sink. Mason jumped out and began to yell at the men as he grabbed the rope. By this time the Jeep was under the water. As he yelled, the men began to help pull and they finally got the Jeep up out of the water.

Poor Jeep! The windshield was flattened onto the hood and there was water in all the gauges, in the oil, in the gas, and everywhere. So Mason sat on the bank of the river to let it dry out in the hot tropical sun. He paid the men, and they gladly went on their way. Many men would probably have hit, kicked, and swore at them; but Mason was just grateful to have the Jeep back. In New Guinea you always carry extra oil and gas, as there are no service stations for hundreds of miles. So after things dried out a bit, Mason drained the oil and gas and replaced them with fresh. The faithful old Jeep started up and Mason drove on home, another four hours.

When he pulled in the driveway in Wau, the family was so happy to see Dad! But all anyone could say was, "What happened to the Jeep?" as they stared at the flattened windshield. There were a lot of stories to tell; but they were all happy ones, as Jesus was with us all the way—including our faithful Jeep that now needed to be repaired.

We now had a clear direction from the Lord, so it was with much excitement that we continued to work on the language and to prepare to move. Mason stripped the jeep down, removing everything that would come off, replaced all bearings, overhauled the motor, and straightened that which was bent. He painted the engine silver and red and the jeep blue with yellow wheels. Now it was ready to roll again.

Virgene and children with our little blue jeep

Preparing to move

Having great faith that we would get the land in the Dunantina Valley, we began to get ready for the move. We knew that we were not going to have electricity out in the jungle, so we began to sell our electrical things—even our lovely hi-fi set we had brought to enjoy our music. We began ordering our anticipated household needs from Australia—a wood burning cookstove, an Electrolux kerosene fridge, and three mattresses. These would be delivered by sea to the coastal port of Madang and then flown over 5,000 feet above sea level to the town of Goroka, where we would pick them up.

We were always grateful that we could plan our family. Now that we knew where we were going to settle and that there would be a hospital three hours away from our new home, we decided to increase our family. When we moved, Virgene was three months pregnant with our fourth child. We were all very happy about this news.

We began making plans for our trip to see and meet the people who we would be able to tell about Jesus and how they could have eternal life. Mason began to inquire about chartering a plane to fly our family and cargo to Goroka. From there we would have a three-hour drive as we traversed the thirty-two miles to the Dunantina Valley.

We were able to purchase a trailer that the Jeep could pull, so Mason planned another trip back up to the valley to take a few things we would need when we arrived and also to arrange to have the bush house enlarged to accommodate our family. After fording rivers, negotiating narrow mountain curves, and avoiding mudslides that often took the entire handmade road away, he arrived safely at Hageri at our "new" but not yet ready home.

He met with the owner concerning the land and showed him

32

how big our bush house would need to be for our family. The existing room was big enough for the kitchen; but we would need to build an additional room big enough for our dining room table and for Bruce's single bed, another room just big enough for our double bed and the girls' three-quarter bed, and a small room to bathe in. Mason had bought nails to help stabilize the structure, as the local people merely tied their houses together with rope vine from the jungle. Our home was to be different than their village huts. Their huts were round and ours was to be square.

Even so, the local people knew how to put it together. First they went into the jungle and cut small trees for the posts of the expansion. Then they took miniature bamboo they grew called pit-pit, cut it, put it on a log, and beat it with a stone until it was flat. Then they wove it into what they called a blind (a wall). This they tied or, in our case, nailed to the posts of the house. The roof was made of long kunai grass made into bundles and layered on several inches thick. The windows were cut out of the blinds, which we propped open in the daytime and closed at night. When the sun went down at 5,500 feet it was cool. The blinds also afforded us some privacy. Mason left the instructions on how to build the house and drove back into Goroka. There he left the Jeep and trailer and flew back to Wau.

WE SEE GOROKA!

The excitement grew as the day drew nearer to fly to Goroka. We had vacated our little rented house in Wau and said our goodbyes to Mr. Schrevaner when we got word that our chartered plane had been canceled until the next day. What a sinking feeling! What should we do? By God's provision the owners of a little hotel just down the road told us to come and stay the night with them. They were the ones who had bought our hi-fi outfit.

The next morning we heard our plane land, and we were ready to get on it. We all were very excited, including Sammy and Judy.

After flying about an hour, we finally saw Goroka, where we landed at the tiny grass strip airport. "We see Goroka!" became a phrase with special meaning for our family over the next many years. The country was so very beautiful with lush green mountains on either side of the winding dirt road leading in and out of town. Waiting for us was our little blue Jeep and our trailer. With the help of some local men, we were so excited to load our necessities for our first night in our new home onto the trailer.

Hageri, our destination, was in an isolated district, thirty-five miles from Goroka. The hand cut dirt roads full of pot-holes and boulders that limited us to twenty to twenty-five miles per hour were nearly impassable, but there was no other way to move the family and our few belongings to our new home. The kids hopped in the metal side seats in the back of the Jeep, with Bruce on one side and Stephanie on the other. We put them on pillows to soften the ride. Sondra sat on Mommy's lap in the front beside Daddy. So with Sammy the dog and Judy the cat and a duck that had been given to us all perched precariously atop the household goods and other luggage, we began our journey. It was a long bumpy ride. Everyone had to brace themselves and hold on, especially Stephanie and Bruce in the back; but we were all so excited it didn't matter. After what seemed a very long time, we came to the Hageri turn off. We knew the road would be bumpy, but we did not have adjectives to describe the five-mile Hageri road where we were fording rivers, crossing small bridges that looked like they would not hold the weight of the Jeep, and going up and down many hills—some frightfully steep.

Encounter with a cannibal chief

"Well, that does it!" Mason exclaimed as he climbed out of the Jeep and surveyed the situation they were in. After three tries of skidding, sliding, and spinning in the muddy red dirt, it became obvious that the Jeep didn't have sufficient power to pull the trailer to the top of a steep grade we were attempting to climb. He knew the hills ahead would be steeper and even more difficult. As he guided the Jeep and trailer back down the slippery slope, the heavily loaded vehicle skidded; and, in spite of his best efforts, it went off the narrow roadway and settled in the soft mud.

The rainy season had already started, and the day before there had been a heavy rain of cloudburst proportions. Standing there on the roadway near the Jeep, Mason was concerned that another storm might break before long. He could see only one option to solve our problem. He turned to Virgene and asked, "Would you and the kids be willing to stay here for a little while?" He went on, "It looks as though I'll have to unhook the trailer and leave you and the children while I take some of the heavier things on to the house. It's only about five miles from here. I should be able to make it there in about thirty minutes. Kiabe will be there and he can help me unload. We'll hurry back just as soon as we can."

Virgene looked around. The setting was calm and road was empty. She didn't see anything or anyone to cause concern. She responded, "Yes, we should be okay. Sure, go ahead. And be sure to take the mattresses on up. If they get wet, we won't have any place to sleep tonight. I hope you make it okay."

Virgene, the children, Sammy, and Judy got out of the Jeep and climbed up on a very big rock. Everything was quiet and peaceful as we watched the blue Jeep carrying Mason and some of our belongings climb up and over the hill. It had just disappeared from sight, when all of a sudden our rock was surrounded by fierce-looking men holding bows and man-killing arrows and stone axes. Bones and shells pierced their noses and ears, and beautifully colored feather headdresses adorned their heads. They wore only a bark loincloth. They just stared at us. We couldn't tell what they were thinking, but they certainly didn't look friendly.

Virgene's heart began to beat very fast, and she began to pray silently. Little Bruce, aware we were in the land of head-hunters, was terrified: "Mommy, are they going to cut our heads off?" Virgene hugged him and the other kids really close and prayed. Then the Lord said to her, "Smile at them!" She answered Bruce, "No, Sweetie, just smile at them." She forced a friendly smile and the children followed suit. The natives then began to jabber in their native language as they talked among themselves. Then they smiled back!

Typical Stone Age warriors

At last we heard the motor of the Jeep and then saw it coming over the hill. What a welcome sight that was! Mason, too, had a shock as he saw his family surrounded by the native men. But with his winning smile, he also won their hearts. They scattered from the area as Mason brought the vehicle to a stop. Kiabe, our interpreter, was with him and spoke to the natives. When Mason and Kiabe took hold of the trailer to get it back on the road, Kiabe called on the natives to help them, and they did.

The chief in charge of what turned out to be a hunting party was Sunupala of the village of Kalikalina. Before we reached our new home, we had come face-to-face with warriors who knew the taste of human flesh. These were the people God had called us to minister to. Sunupala's story is told in more detail in chapter 7.

Buckingham Palace

We all climbed back into the Jeep, and with the lightened trailer in tow, we made it up and over the hills to arrive at our new home. We all cheered Daddy, who had done such a good job driving. We stood and looked at the little bush house; it was perfect. (Our first visitor from the U.S. would name it Buckingham Palace.) Because the children would be on the floor a lot, Mason had asked the builders to make matting from bamboo to cover the gravelly, uneven dirt floor. The matting was also a wonderful blessing as we put our mattresses on the floor. We had a little kerosene one-burner stove that we cooked on.

Buckingham Palace; our first bush home

There was a lot left for Mason to do, but we did have a helper. On the house-hunting trip when Mason had shown the men how he wanted the house built, Kiabe—one of the two that spoke New Guinea Pidgin—was there. Mason had asked him if he would like to work for us and help with whatever we needed to have done. Kiabe was honored to be asked. He was thrilled to serve us, and we were grateful for his help. But Mason could never remember his name, so he gave him the name of Sam. He has kept that name to this day.

To make our home more comfortable and useable, we still needed to build the beds and table and make kitchen cabinets. To make the cabinet, Mason took the wooden crate in which the fridge had come and cut it in half. He then put shelves in it to hold our dishes and pans. He also had a very unnerving task of installing our wood burning cook stove. How could a stovepipe be run safely through a grass roof? He asked the Lord to give him wisdom. On a trip to Goroka, he bought three sizes of graduated metal pipe and ran them through each other. He then put another piece of metal around the pipe at the grass roof. And we prayed. We lived in that bush house nearly nine months and never had a fire, except in the stove. The Lord is gracious and worthy to be praised!

What about water and other facilities? Not far from the house we had a path that split into a Y about half way along it. One leg led to the outhouse and the other leg to a spring. We did have to share the spring with the village pigs— but it was water! Needless to say, we boiled all of our drinking water until our own metal water tank was made. On one of his trips to Goroka, Mason brought back metal material that he soldered together to make our water tank, which we used to catch water from our roof. We often bathed right across the road in Dunantina River. It was large enough to swim in. We washed clothes in a large tub like grandmother used to have. We also could use it for bathing. By American standards we were living under most primitive conditions. But by New Guinea standards, the luxuries we enjoyed were beyond belief.

We were at our new home for only a few hours, when the word began to spread: "The white family is here!" Some had heard our Jeep. From that day on we had hundreds of people standing around our house from sunup to sundown. Each morning when the shutters in our kitchen and dining room were lifted, a yard full of natives pressed close to gape in astonishment at our strange ways. They had never seen things like what we had in our house. They had never seen a metal saucepan; their dishes were made of clay. They had never seen people put food on a plate; they had only one wooden dish for the village. They had never seen anyone cook on a stove; they had a fire on the dirt floor in the middle of their hut. Although this constant scrutiny was something of a nuisance and definitely an invasion of privacy, we soon realized that we were affording the natives an opportunity to learn of a new way of life.

Chapter 4
SOME FIRSTS IN THE
DUNANTINA VALLEY

The Spirit of the Lord is upon me, because he hath
anointed me to preach the gospel to the poor; he
hath sent me to heal the brokenhearted, to preach
deliverance to the captives, and recovering of sight
to the blind, to set at liberty them that are bruised,
To preach the acceptable year of the Lord.
—LUKE 4:18–19, KJV

W HEN THE FINAL decision had been made to locate in the
Dunantina Valley, Mason felt that he should select his
interpreter and helper from among the young men of
the area. Kiabe's qualifications far exceeded the others. The fact
that he had spent two years working in coastal towns gave him
some knowledge and understanding of the outside world. And
most importantly, he knew the language we had learned, New
Guinea Pidgin.

FIRST CONVERT, KIABE (SAM)

We felt it was very important for Kiabe to have a saving
knowledge of Jesus Christ, so that he would be able to translate our message to the natives with both mental and spiritual
understanding. One day when Mason was working in the garden
with him, he brought up the subject, "Kiabe, you need to know
firsthand what you are talking about when you translate for me.

Would you be willing to accept Jesus as your Savior and let Him change your life?" Kiabe's response was immediate and sincere, "Yes! How do I do this?" Mason explained the way of salvation from the Scripture. Then Kiabe followed him in praying the sinner's prayer: "Jesus, I have sinned and I am sorry for my sins. Please forgive me. I believe You are the only Savior. Come into my heart, Lord Jesus, and set me free." Kiabe was immediately filled with joy that comes only from God. He began to grow and mature in his faith. Kiabe's changed life interested and impacted many people.

He was so proud when Mason gave him a new name, Sam, and we took him to live at the mission to serve as our interpreter (turntalk) and our houseboy. We built him a small hut near ours. He was a trusted and faithful part of our ministry for many years.

Sam's faith triumphant

Although he had been set free from sin, Sam was still afraid of the witch doctors who had held his tribesmen in bondage for years. It was through fear that the witch doctors ruled the people. Sam had a terrible fear of a certain area that had been used many times as a battleground. Because many warriors had been killed there, the natives thought that their spirits still inhabited the place. Sam was afraid that the spirits would bring him harm if he walked near this battleground. Mason knew that Sam needed to gain victory over this superstition and his fear of the witch doctors. He assured him that when he accepted Christ as his Savior and He came to live in his heart, he no longer needed to fear the spirits of the dead anymore. He also told him that the witch doctor could no longer put a curse on him and he no longer needed to fear him. He reminded him that he was now God's child and shared the scripture in

1 John 4:4: "Ye are of God, little children, and have overcome them: because greater is he that is in you, than he that is in the world." He also told him that "Christ has promised to give you authority 'over all the power of the enemy, and nothing shall by any means hurt you'" (Luke 10:19).

Then Mason spoke directly, "Because Christ dwells in your heart, Sam, you have more power than the witch doctor and the spirits of the dead cannot harm you. You don't have to fear the witch doctor, and you no longer need to be frightened when you go near the old battleground." So Mason walked with Sam through the battleground to prove to himself that Jesus Christ in his heart is stronger and greater than all the power of the enemy. Sam was victorious; he had won his first battle against Satan.

Although we did not learn about it until many months later, Sam's newfound faith was again put to the test. The witch doctors were angry because Sam had left the old ways and accepted the new religion and our new way of life. A group of men including the witch doctor came down out of the hills. They saw Sam working for us and how happy he was. He had his own little grass hut, he wore clothes, he ate good food, and he enjoyed working for us. They were upset and jealous. They wanted Sam to return to his village and embrace the old ways again.

Sam told them no. He loved us and knew we needed him; he was not at all interested in moving backward. They were outraged! This young man was defying them, something they had not experienced before. They threatened him, "You'll be sorry. We'll put a curse upon you!" Sam was well aware of the ramifications of what they were saying, but he was no longer ruled by fear.

They went back to the bush. Sam grew up under the power of the witch doctor. With his potions and incantations he could cause a person many miles away to get sick and even die a miserable death. People would suddenly die even though medical doctors could find nothing wrong with them. They would die in the same way and at the same time the witch doctor told them. These superstitions affected the native's ability to think for themselves. They did not question the witch doctor's authority, fully believing that any curse that was placed upon them could never be revoked. It was a life of fear.

Sam had been delivered from this fear by his faith in Jesus Christ. He believed Mason's words and the Word of God that told him he had Someone within him whose power was greater than that of the witch doctor. Sam prayed and fasted and trusted the Lord.

Back in the bush the witch doctor was busy with his potions and curses. When it came time for Sam to be very sick for no apparent reason, men were sent to check on him and see how he was doing. They checked his house expecting him to be very ill on his bed, but he wasn't there. Then they came to our home. They looked in through our open windows and saw Sam happily walking around and singing as he worked—well and normal. They were very frightened.

They ran back to the bush to report their findings to the witch doctor. For the first time the medicine of the witch doctor had failed. He was put to shame before the whole village. They realized that the "Man" Sam had found had something greater and more powerful than they had. They were afraid Sam might use this power to come and destroy them.

Sam wasn't interested in destroying them—he wanted them to share in the new life he had found. The power of God had triumphed over the power of witchcraft. Sam interpreted Mason as he told and retold the wonderful stories of Jesus and His power to save men from their sins and give them authority over all the power of the enemy, including the witch doctor.

FIRST SERVICE AND MORE

Shortly after we arrived, we had our first church service in front of our house with some 100 people gathered, all sitting or squatting on the ground. Squatting was fine with them for that was all they knew; they didn't have any furniture in their houses.

First church service in front of Buckingham Palace

The next Sunday we had two to three times as many people, so we moved to the side of the house up on a little hill. More kept coming each Sunday. They were not sure when Sunday was as they had no calendar or clocks, but word would soon spread when we told Sam, "Tomorrow is Sunday." Each Sunday the numbers grew until there were several hundred.

Mason faithfully preached the message of the love of God offered to them through His Son, Jesus Christ, and shared the fascinating stories of the Bible; all interpreted by Sam. But to the natives that was all they were, just interesting stories.

First Christmas

The year was coming to an end and Christmas was very near. It would often take three months for a package to come from the United States. Even so, we decided to make our purchases from the Sears and Montgomery Ward catalogs, as there were few toys available in the little grocery store in Goroka. The kids were young and did not know when Christmas really would be according to the calendar. So, when the orders arrived just a couple weeks after Christmas, Daddy went out and brought back a Christmas tree. Our children thoroughly enjoyed their first Christmas in New Guinea. Of course there were no lights on the tree, but that was okay with them. Only Stephanie was old enough to remember Christmas in America.

The natives thought we were really strange—these white people bringing a tree into the house! This gave us a great opportunity to tell them the story of Jesus' birth and how God gave to them His only Son that they could have eternal life in heaven. But it was still only a story to them.

School for Stephanie

Even though Stephanie would not be six until the first of April, we wanted to start her with the Australian school year, which went from the second week of January until the first week of December. We had American missionary friends who had their children enrolled in a free Australian correspondence course from Queensland, with which they were quite happy. Virgene was nervous about having the full responsibility of our children's education on her shoulders. This program was set up so that the child's work would be returned each week to a qualified teacher who would then examine and return it. This made

Virgene feel more confident. Mason made Stephanie a neat little desk with a top that rose up where she could keep her books.

This is when obedience had to take place. We had already trained the people, with Sam's help, to go away from the house while we ate. Since they had never had baths, the aroma and flies surrounding them made this mealtime separation necessary. By this time they were good on their own during mealtime, but not being able to stand at the windows to watch us during the day was another issue! Sam did his best to explain Stephanie's schooling and why they had to be quiet.

The school schedule was rigid, every morning from 8:00 to 12:00 noon. The curious natives were quite impressed with the importance we placed on the schooling of our child. It was obvious to them that we considered Stephanie's schooling a matter of first importance. Nothing stopped the lessons. They wanted to know what the stick was in Stephanie's hand and how it could make a mark on the paper. Also, what was this book and what was she doing with it? They had only seen a Bible during church time.

When Stephanie finished her day of school, she would get the chiefs and others and line them up on a big log in the yard and make them say their ABCs. It was so cute to watch. It wasn't long before a delegation of chiefs came and talked to Mason. They asked, "Would it be possible for us to have a school?" The natives were beginning to realize that we enjoyed a much better way of life than they did. And like parents the world over, they wanted their children to have opportunities such as they themselves had never dreamed of having.

At first we thought that such an undertaking would be utterly impossible. But as time went by, we saw the need for this school and realized that it would help us in evangelizing these people.

So we began to write down the names of the children whose parents wanted to enter them in school. However, the actual opening of the school had to wait until we could put up a building and that would be a couple of years away.

First full moon

The mission work was growing and Mason was getting more invitations to come to the villages. The villages were farther and farther away. For one trip he decided to stay for three days. Up until this time Virgene had not stayed alone with the children, but she knew that Jesus was with them all. We said good-bye to Daddy and watched the blue Jeep disappear over the hill.

Virgene began to teach Stephanie while Bruce and Sondra played outside. Sam came and said that Bai, an assistant chief from a village a few miles away named Nakento, wanted to talk to her. Virgene told him to wait a few minutes until Stephanie had her recess, and then she would talk to him. When the time came, she asked Sam to find Bai and he found that he had gone back to the village. She felt badly, but knew he would come back. Throughout the busy day, she forgot about Bai.

After dinner she tucked the children in and went to bed. Before she could get to sleep, she began to hear the native drums. Her first thought was that Bai was cross with her and that they were coming down to the house. She was afraid at first. Then she began to pray that the Lord would take her fear away and protect her and the children. She was then able to fall asleep.

When she awoke the next morning, she heard Sam making a fire in the stove. She quickly dressed and went out to ask about the drums the night before. Sam smiled and said, "Oh Misses (Pidgin for a white woman), it is the full moon and the people always play their drums, sing, and dance when there is a full moon." That was a lesson well learned and with it came an opportunity to draw a bit closer to Jesus.

First tribal war

Another time God's protection was evident wasn't long after we arrived. We heard a big commotion. We asked Sam what was going on. He told us, "Oh, two tribes are fighting over the bridge and they are fighting over land up on the road." Mason, always ready to assist, responded, "Oh, I'll go up and see if I can help." Virgene reacted strongly, "Oh, no! You stay right here!" Mason countered, "I'll go up in the Jeep. That way I can get away quickly if necessary." Virgene prayed fervently for his protection.

It was a fight that had erupted quickly, so the natives did not have their bows and arrows, which was unusual. They were using stones and clubs. Mason spoke to them through Sam as he tried to quiet them. He finally got them to agree to have Ross, the patrol officer, look at his maps and see where the right boundaries were. The people promised not to fight any more and wait and see what Ross would say. Soon Mason came back down the hill with two men in the Jeep. He said, "These are the two chiefs, and I am going to take them to Henganofi to get Ross to settle the difference. Virgene retorted, "Oh, no! You are not going to leave the kids and me here alone when they are still very cross!" So we all jumped in the Jeep and traveled the hour to get to the patrol post. We left Sam to watch over the house.

When we got to Henganofi and Mason told Ross the story, he said, "Oh, come on in and have a cup of tea." Though it was lunch time and we were hungry, we were confused and slightly perturbed to be invited for a cup of tea when there had just been a fight right by our house. We were learning what Ross already knew about these people. After a leisurely visit and cup of tea, he told us to take the two chiefs back and that he would be along later and settle the dispute.

When we got back home, there were the disputing tribes squatting around our house, one tribe on one side and the other tribe on the other side. Wow! When the two chiefs got out of the Jeep, they each told their tribes what Ross had said. Even so, the angry faces on either side of us made it obvious there was still hostility and tension between the two groups. We were at a loss as to why Ross had not come quickly.

As the afternoon wore on, natives from first one group and then the other would get up and straggle off over the hills. They had had no lunch, and no doubt they were hungry. When Ross finally arrived, most of the natives had gone. They had tired of waiting. "Just as I expected," he chuckled.

There were injuries during the fight, some so serious that they had to be taken to the hospital in Goroka. The government imposed a stiff penalty on the tribes who broke the peace. Thirty-five men from each group were fined and given a six-month jail sentence. As the jail at Henganofi was too small to hold that many prisoners, they were sent to work on a road that was being built in another district. This may have been a blessing in disguise, for it gave these men a chance to travel and see new things beyond their own narrow valley and an opportunity to broaden their vision and understanding.

Later Ross arranged a meeting with the two tribes and brought his maps to show them just where the boundary between them should be. They accepted his decision without further ado. We lived and learned.

Being that New Guinea was the most primitive country in the world, the people still practiced headhunting and cannibalism in several areas. Because of this custom, people remained within the confines of their village. Each village had their own tribal marks on their face. When they were out hunting, these marks identified someone as friend or foe. Often they would kill if you were not from their area. The men's communal huts often had human skulls hanging from the thatched roof to signify their victories. They often would eat their enemies and their own dead as well. They knew no other way of life. That is what made them very territorial and why they were a warring people and did not know peace.

First Visitor and New Babies

Mason made trips to Goroka every ten days or so, but Virgene and the children went only every six weeks to two months or when she needed her prenatal check up because the six-hour trip was very hard. This was always a special time of fellowship that we treasured, as we sat under a tree eating a cheese sandwich for lunch and had a time of sharing the hard times and the encouraging times. Besides, it was nice to see some white faces of other missionaries that were in town for their supplies. There were only a few missionary couples in the area. When we passed their turn off, we knew by the tire tracks which family we would be seeing in town. In our isolated mountain area, it made no difference what organization or denomination the missionaries were from. We all helped each other and appreciated the encouragement and friendship we shared. Along our thirty-five mile trip, there was one mountaintop from which we could finally see Goroka. The kids would always get so excited, and we would hear "I See Goroka" chanted for the next half hour.

One day when Mason arrived home from Goroka, he was

very excited. We had a letter from our Foursquare Missions office saying that Dr. Harold Chalfant was coming to New Guinea to visit us. What a privilege! He was the one who had challenged Mason to fill out the application to come to the mission field. We polished up the bush house as much as we could. We put Bruce in our bedroom so Harold could use Bruce's bed in the dining room.

Mason's heart was beating fast as he saw the DC-3 land on the grass airstrip. Then he saw Harold's smiling face coming down the plane steps. How wonderful to see someone from "home"! After we hugged and put his suitcase in the Jeep, the first thing Harold said was, "Mason, don't feed me anything you would not eat." Mason said, "No worries." The plane had come in at about 4 p.m. So, aware that Harold would be hungry before we made our three-hour drive, Mason had bought him a lovely Cadbury's chocolate bar with nuts in it. We always loved them. Before we got started, Mason gave the candy bar to Harold informing him of the three-hour trip and that he didn't want him to get hungry. When Harold opened the candy bar, worms were crawling all over it. Mason apologized, wanting to crawl under the Jeep. You never know in the tropics what you are going to see or get. Harold handled it okay, but he was hungry before we got home. He was absolutely taken in with the primitiveness of the country and the people and also their lack of clothing.

It seemed like a long day before Virgene and the children heard the Jeep coming over the hill. We were so excited. As soon as our greetings were made, immediately Harold said, "Have you named your house?" We said, "No, we had not thought of that with so much going on." He said, "I want to name it Buckingham Palace." We were all delighted with such a fitting name for our little bush house.

We were glad Sam had dinner all ready because everyone was starved. We sat down to eat our freshly prepared spaghetti. As we passed Harold the Parmesan cheese and he shook it onto his spaghetti, a cockroach came flying out! Evidently Sam had forgotten to close the top. Oh my, what to do? What a welcome Harold had—first with the worms on the candy bar and now the cockroach!

As night fell we showed Harold where he would sleep in the living room, gave him a flashlight (torch), and showed him the "path." It was bedtime and we were all tired, so we said good-night. The next morning Sam came to build the fire. He did not see Harold, for he had risen very early and gone for a walk. Soon the people began to gather around the house. He was amazed and asked, "Is it always like this?" We told him to just wait, it was still early. By breakfast time he could hardly speak, he was so amazed to see all the people gathered around our house. From then on he was busy all day taking pictures, both still shots and video. Mason took him in several directions, and he was just speechless as he saw the people—the men with their beautiful feather headdresses, bones and shells through their nose, ears, etc., and the women and the little girls always with only their bark skirts no matter how tiny they were, and the little boys with no clothing.

One day we all sat down to talk. Harold said, "Well, Mason and Virgene, I cannot believe how well you have settled in with the most primitive people I have ever seen, and I have been in many, many countries. I know God is going to bless you and prosper the work of God. Also, one message that the Mission Board asked me to give to all the missionaries is not to have too many children. But I think I am a little late here." We all laughed, as our fourth baby was due in a few weeks.

We had a wonderful time with Harold. What a blessing to have our first visitor, especially from the U.S.! He told us his visit had set his heart on fire for missions. We prayed, said our good-byes, and then Virgene and the children watched the blue Jeep go over the hill.

Oh! Here comes the baby...and then another

Just a couple weeks after our visit from Dr. Chalfant, Virgene woke up about 3:00 a.m. on a Sunday morning with labor pains. She quietly got up and went out to light the kerosene stove to heat up some water so she could wash up a little. Of course, Mason heard her and came rushing out. We got the children up and started our three-hour trip to Goroka. By the time we made the long bumpy trip, the pains had vanished. But when the doctor saw Virgene, he said, "You cannot go back out. You must stay in town." Thank the Lord there was a Christian couple from Australia living in Goroka who had offered their guest room if we needed it. Yes, we needed it.

Mason took Stephanie, Bruce, and Sondra back home. Our neighbors, the Kingsford Smiths—coffee owners five miles up the road, had offered to keep the children. We were so glad that we had Sam and that we could trust him to look after the house.

Before Mason had left Goroka, he had gone to the post office where he found a box from his parents. Of course the kids could hardly wait to get home to open it. There were a lot of goodies, plus a small American flag. Bruce fell in love with the flag and carried it everywhere he went. Later in the day Mason heard a curdling yell, "Daddy, come and help me!" It was coming from the end of the path! He ran as fast as he could, wondering what he was going to find! When he opened the door of the outhouse, Bruce was crying heart-broken tears. He managed to get the words out between sobs, "Daddy, I dropped the flag down the hole. Please get it!" Daddy explained as sweetly as he could that he would not be able to retrieve the flag. He quickly added that we would ask Grandpa and Grandma to send another one.

At long last on May 16, tiny Michele Irene came into this world at 5 pounds and 10 ounces with blonde hair, blue eyes, and very fair skin, just like her daddy. The doctor, an Australian, wanted us to stay in Goroka to rest for ten days after the birth. He warned us not to let the people touch her as they never washed their hands and had many diseases because of this. We kept that in mind. Finally the big day came when we started home with our new baby. A few months before, two or three men from the coast had come through our area selling beautiful woven baskets, so we ordered a big one to use for a bassinet when our baby would arrive. We put a pillow in the basket to cushion our little girl for her three-hour ride home.

Everything went well until we were about half way up the Hageri road. We came over a hill to find a human chain of natives blockading the road. We looked at each other, worried and thinking this must be another tribal fight. Mason stopped the Jeep and asked what the problem was. The men said, "Oh, no problem! We just want to see the white baby." That was a relief! From then on we would have many who would walk long distances over many mountain ranges to see the *white baby*. To the dark-skinned natives, she was an amazing sight.

(Later, when we were in the Philippines for a couple of years filling in for missionary who was on leave, God gave us another beautiful baby girl—Denise Lynne, born May 11, 1963. We then had five children—three Americans, one New Guinean, and now a Filipino! Our quiver was full.)

Hughes family, 1966 (left to right—back row: Bruce and Sondra; middle row: Stephanie, Virgene, Mason, and Michele; front row: Denise)

FIRST WARRIOR CONVERT

As we continued our Sunday services on the hillside by the house, the numbers continued to grow. Sam would interpret what Mason was saying to the natives. But these words and these concepts were all new to them. Who is this Jesus? Who is this God? Each time Mason asked them if they wanted to take Jesus into their heart, there was a lot of talking but no response. So, we just kept praying that soon they would comprehend and want to receive Jesus into their hearts.

Finally, one Sunday as Mason gave God's Word and again asked if anyone would like to have Jesus in their heart, one man stood up. He told us, "I want to try this thing that you have been telling us about." Our hearts leaped with joy! With his bow and man-killing arrows held tightly in his hands, bones and shells in his nose and ears, his hair greasy and matted, and only his bark loin cloth covering him, he wanted Jesus. Mason asked him to come down to the front. As Mason prayed in Pidgin and Sam interpreted, this man repeated Sam's words in his native language and asked Jesus to forgive him and come into his heart. Later we found out his name was Tabiak. We rejoiced with all of our hearts. We had our first convert!

A few mornings later when we got up, Sam had opened the shutters in the kitchen and living area and built a fire in the woodstove. When we walked into the kitchen from our bedroom (understandably, we had no shutters in the bedroom), we saw a man squatting out in the yard. He was bathed, wore clothes, had clean hair that was neatly cut, and he carried neither bow nor arrows. We thought we had a visitor from somewhere else. We said to Sam, "Who is this who has come to visit us?" He smiled and said, "That is Tabiak." He had been cleansed inside by the saving blood of Jesus, but he also wanted to be clean outside. We were all amazed at his transformation! More of Tabiak's story is told in chapter 7.

It wasn't long before the good news spread of how Tabiak had changed inside as well as outside. More began to accept Jesus at each service. Also chiefs from other villages came with invitations to come to their village and tell their people about "this Jesus." When Mason would leave for a village, Sam would have to go with him to interpret. Of course that would leave Virgene without an interpreter, but she did okay.

Kiabe (Sam) and Mason preaching in a village

First Village Convert, the Guinea Pig

Mason had a real desire to go from the main mission station to a village, so after much prayer we chose a village about forty-five minutes down the road named Kenemoti. No one from this area had ever come to the mission at Hageri.

Mason went once a week for about six months, but no one would respond to give their heart to Jesus. It was time to go again; and he said to Virgene, "I don't think I will go any more. After all, the Lord told us if they won't hear you, shake the dust off your feet and move on (Matt. 10:14)." Well, there certainly was plenty of dust to do that! Virgene responded with the wisdom of the Holy Spirit, "How will they know you are not coming? After all, you have been teaching them integrity. Why don't you go and tell them you are not going to come any more; give it another week or so."

Mason realized her advice was good (as always), so he went again to the village and preached Jesus to them. At the close of his message, as always, he invited anyone who was willing to step out and follow the Lord. Again, as always, they began to talk among themselves. But, this time one man stood up and came and stood before him—feathers in his hair, bone and shells in his nose and ears, a stone ax in his string woven waist band, and bow and man-killing arrows in his hand. He looked Mason in the eye, and said, "I am here to try what you have been talking about."

Headhunter with man-killing arrows

Well, Mason, still young, thought, "I have never had anyone want to receive Christ on a trial basis. Perhaps you better wait a while." But the thought was immediately interrupted by the inner voice of the Holy Spirit, "How long have you been coming here?" Mason responded in his spirit, "About six months." The voice of the Spirit went on, "And why have you come?" Again Mason's inner man responded, "I want them to receive Jesus as their Savior." The Lord replied, "You have a man standing in front of you. What is your problem?" The message was clear: "Thank You, Lord!"

Mason turned to his interpreter and said, "Tell him to repeat this prayer from his mouth and heart." Mason led him in a prayer of repentance and acceptance, which the interpreter translated so the man could pray with understanding. The villager went back and joined the others from his tribe, and Mason went home.

When he arrived home, Virgene immediately asked, "Did you tell them that you are not coming anymore?" Mason replied, "No." She pressed further, "Why not? Did someone accept Jesus?" He responded, "Well, I guess so." Again the Lord spoke to Mason's spirit man, "What does My Word say?" (Romans 10:9: "If you confess with your mouth the Lord Jesus and believe in your heart that God has raised Him from the dead, you will be saved.") Convicted of the truth of the matter, Mason turned back to Virgene and said, "Yes, we had our first convert today."

The next week when Mason went down to Kenemoti he saw the new convert. He was all cleaned up, he had removed his man-killing arrows from the rest of his arrows, and he was very happy. He told Mason his story: Every time you came and asked someone to receive Jesus, all the villagers were afraid what would happen to them if they give their heart to a Man or invited that Man into their life. So, I said to them, 'I will go and try it. You can watch me and decide for yourself what you want to do.'" The life of this new convert, his speech and everything, had all changed. This people seeing this change in his life decided they wanted to receive this Man Jesus into their hearts also. Mason found out the name of the new convert was Marari. He discipled

Marari and he became one of the strong pastors of his tribe and a wonderful Christian man.

The moral of this story is that the enemy had an idea of what might happen if his stronghold in this village was broken, so he tried to discourage Mason from continuing. But God had a strong backup for him (thank the Lord for a wonderful spirit-filled wife).

It wasn't long after that, however, that the witch doctor threatened the people and the pastor if they did not return back to their old way. But Marari remembered the Word of God Mason had given him: "You are of God, little children, and have overcome them, because He who is in you is greater than he who is in the world" (1 John 4:4). And this included all witch doctors. He told the witch doctor, "I am no longer afraid of you. Do what you will." This angered the witch doctor very much. He tried to work double evil on this group of people; but after a few days he saw for the first time in his life that his power was not working. It had no effect on those people and their pastor. The people of the village mocked him. He was afraid and ran out of the village, calling back to them, "Don't work your power on me!"

Nakento boy's curse lifted

Assistant Chief Bai's village of Nakento was one of the first villages where Mason began to hold services, about five miles on up the valley. This is the story of a young boy at Nakento. Mason would always go up the road to Nakento on Wednesdays, only about a forty-minute drive. It was a very rough road because of the many rivers we had to cross. This day it had been raining, the road was very muddy with some landslides. We experienced an abnormal amount of difficulty getting across the first river. Once we got across we continued

61

on to the second river, which we could not negotiate at all because the water was running unusually swift. So we parked the Jeep and pondered a new course of action. We were told if we went up to a small break in the river, we would come to some large rocks we could use to negotiate a river crossing. So we decided to walk up river and find these huge rocks that we could use to cross. We trekked up the riverbank quite a long way and came upon the big rocks. Remember, this is mountain country. New Guinea is 60 percent mountains, and we are in the Dunantina Valley where the water comes gushing from both sides of the mountain ranges and drains into the valley—often washing away small trees and shrubs. Although the waters this day were very swift and the current was abnormally strong, we managed to jump on these big rocks to get across the raging river. After that, it was just a short distance to Nakento where we had planned to have the meeting.

When we got there, the village was in a great uproar. Mason began to inquire about this unusual commotion. Sam spoke to the villagers and explained to Mason that a mother of the village had died and they buried her at a little place atop a mountain. Before she died she had told her young son, "I will not let you leave me. You will stay with me forever." Sam told Mason that this young boy was physically unable to leave her burial site. If he tried to leave, something would choke him with a feeling like hands around his neck so he could not breathe. This forced him to turn back and stay. All of the people were agitated about this and discussing what should be done. It was then that Mason realized why the enemy had tried to keep him from coming. The enemy had caused all these unusual challenges that we had experienced along the way, but the Lord enabled us to prevail and had won out over the enemy.

Mason knew exactly what was wrong with this young boy. He had a curse put upon him by his mother. Mason also knew that Jesus could break the power of that curse. He said to the people, "Bring him here so that I can pray for him. Jesus has the power to relieve him of this curse. This is the only way he will be able to leave that burial site." They replied, "No, we have tried and tried and he will not leave that burial site. When he tries, his breath is taken and he begins to choke." Mason responded, "Well, let us pray." He wanted these people to see what the power of Jesus was like, so he said, "Let's release the power of God right now so that he can come to us. When he gets here amongst his own people, we will pray for him and he will be totally set free." So Mason prayed, "Lord Jesus, I ask You right now to release this young boy so that he can come here and we can pray a prayer of deliverance over this curse."

After this prayer the villagers walked to the gravesite. They said to the child, "Come! The missionary wants to talk to you." The young boy said, "I cannot." They said, "Yes, you can. He says you can. Just try it." So the boy began walking slowly and discovered he wasn't being choked. He continued to walk right out of the area. He no longer felt any hands around his neck and he was able to breathe. So he came into the village where the church was. Mason explained to the boy what the problem was and how the enemy had caused that to happen. He explained to them all how the power of Jesus was greater than the power of the enemy. He used 1 John 4:4: "You are of God, little children, and have overcome them, because He who is in you is greater than he who is in the world."

Mason asked the little boy, "Are you a Christian?" The child responded, "No." He explained to the boy, "You need to have Jesus Christ as your Savior. Would you like to become a

Christian?" The boy nodded, "Yes." So Mason led him in prayer through Sam and that little boy wholeheartedly received Jesus Christ as his Savior. Then Mason prayed a prayer of deliverance that he would be delivered totally and completely from the curse that his mother had placed upon him. He was instantly delivered.

The people in that village and in that church began to rejoice. They had just witnessed the power of God through answered prayer. And that was just the beginning. They witnessed many more miracles of God as they prayed over many trials and tribulations. This young boy's experience built their faith, and it built their understanding that they serve a God that is all-powerful. God is more powerful than any curse that can be placed upon anyone. He is more powerful than any happening that the witch doctor controls and tries to bring upon them. They eagerly embraced the truth that they were free, in the name of Jesus and because of the blood of Jesus Christ, to defeat the enemy. So that is the miracle of a young man in the village of Nakento. Praise God for the power of prayer.

Hissing snakes

One day Assistant Chief Bai came to our house for his daily visit. Sam told us to come and look at Bai. He was hissing like a snake and could not talk. We knew this was an attack of Satan through his demons. We prayed for him and he was immediately delivered. Then in a few minutes another man came also hissing. Later that afternoon another man came hissing like snake. Mason began to pray, as he realized the demon had gone from one person to another. As he prayed, God said to him very distinctly, "Pray over this man and tell the demon to go to his place." As he did this, everyone was delivered. We praised God anew for His power over the witch doctor and his demons.

Chapter 5
SPIRITUAL MISSIONARIES

*Then I heard the Lord asking, "Whom should I send
as a messenger to this people? Who will go for us?" I
said, "Here I am. Send me." And he said, "Yes, go, and
say to this people, 'Listen carefully....Watch closely.'"*
—ISAIAH 6:8–9, NLT

W E SPOKE IN chapter 2 of how, during our original
journey across the Pacific, we began to talk and plan
our missionary strategy. What kind of missionaries we
would be? Our experience with missions and missionaries was
somewhat limited. We had heard of medical missionaries who
primarily addressed medical concerns, missionaries whose main
ministry was teaching school, missionaries who helped with
building or agricultural projects, etc. We agreed together, "No,
we are not going to be any of these. We are just going to preach
the gospel." Well, we had to "eat our words" when we began to
minister to the people. The people in Highlands of New Guinea
had needs in all of those areas. The Lord brought us to them to
preach His gospel, and we did that faithfully; but our ministry to
their physical and other needs would authenticate the words we
were telling them about a God who loved them and cared about
them. To be true "spiritual" missionaries, we needed to minister
to them in all those areas and do all of those things we said we
wouldn't do—medical, building, agricultural, teaching in many

areas including school, and many other things. Our lives needed to demonstrate what our mouths were speaking.

MEDICAL

As we looked at the people who stood around our house all day from morning till night, our hearts would go out to them. Some had big burns; as they slept on the dirt floor, sometimes they would roll over into the fire, which they kept burning all night to keep warm for they had no blankets. Many had sores on their skin, especially scabies, a skin disease caused by a little mite and spread by close skin-to-skin contact, made worse by poor hygiene. These people had never had a bath or a shampoo in their lives. The people had absolutely no knowledge of sanitation and how the swarms of flies around them caused the spread of many of their diseases. Many, especially babies, had pneumonia and many had dysentery. Malaria was a big killer because of the dense mosquito population. Our hearts went out to them. So, Mason got a book on medicine and then he bought bandages and other simple things when he would go to town. Soon we had long lines of people waiting for us to help them with their medical needs using only the simple things we had.

Before long it became too expensive to continue to buy the needed supplies with our small stipend. So Mason went to the small hospital in Goroka. The hospital for the expatriates was a converted two-bedroom house with beds. The native hospital for the indigenous people was made up of two or three large kuni grass structures with no rooms and makeshift beds. The beds consisted of boards supported on sawhorses about three feet apart. There were two rows of beds in each structure.

Mason found a doctor and told him what he was doing. The doctor responded, "That is great! You come in next week and spend three days with me, and I will give you a crash course on tropical medicine. After that I'll give you all the supplies you need." That was music to our ears. So we set the time and went back. The doctor taught Mason how to give injections of penicillin and other things. Mason had only followed him around for three hours when the doctor said, "You already know all I can teach you." Mason seemed to have an aptitude for the medical work. The doctor loaded him up with supplies. Mason was so happy when he arrived back at Buckingham Palace.

At that time Virgene had developed a tropical ulcer, another common malady, so she was Mason's guinea pig, his first patient to whom he gave an injection. From then on we spent many hours helping the people. Since the natives had never had medicine of any kind, they responded quickly to penicillin and other modern drugs. The news of Mason's medical work spread through the mountains quickly. Sometimes people came from far away villages he had never visited to receive medical attention. Beside diseases there were injuries caused by the dangers of the jungle or from tribal wars. He cleaned and dressed what wounds he could. Other more serious wounds that might need surgery were usually taken to the government hospital. We also taught them about cleanliness and sanitation, and health conditions began to improve.

The medical work was time consuming and exhausting and limited our time and energy to do "spiritual" ministry. But the Lord knew what He was doing, as always. Even though there was a language barrier, the people understood our caring touches and friendly smiles. We were able to give them relief for problems for which the witch doctor had no cure. The natives were grateful for our care and help. This helped to build their trust in us. Much prayer went up to God when giving any type of medicine to the local people. They lived by the law of an eye for an eye and a tooth for a tooth—payback. If they died soon after I gave them an injection or any medicine, it could cost me my life or the life of one of my family members.

God heals babies and saves grandpa

The rainy season began, which made the grass roof of the house very damp. We did our best to keep our tiny baby Michele warm. But she had pneumonia twice before she was six months old. We were glad that Daddy had the training to give her the penicillin injections.

One day when she was very sick, Tubabufa, the chief from our nearest village, came to the door and said, "Matrapa, can you come and give our baby a shot? (Matrapa was the name the natives called Mason, meaning "the friendly white man who always waves.") Mason asked what was wrong with the baby. He said, "She is breathing just like your baby." He could see Michele's heavy breathing.

So Mason took his little medical box, and they both jumped in the Jeep. They drove for about twenty minutes and then had to walk about half an hour longer to get to the village. When he got to the hut and opened the box, Mason realized he had left the syringes on the stove to sterilize. He knew a runner could go more quickly than he could drive, so he wrote a note to Virgene on a piece of gauze wrapping telling her he needed a syringe and sent the runner on his way.

God works in mysterious ways and accomplishes His work! While the runner was gone, Mason talked to the people of the village. He saw an old man whom he had not seen come down to church. He found out that he was Tubabufa's father. The old man said, "No, I have killed many people down there. Their spirits are still walking around and they will get me if I come down." Mason told him about Jesus, His love, and His great power over all the spirits. The old man took Jesus into his heart right then. Then he said, "I sleep cold at night. I hear that you have blankets. Could you give me one?" Mason asked the Holy Spirit to give him wisdom, for he knew if he gave one a blanket, a thousand more would want one. So he said to the old man, "You come to church next Sunday and I will give you a blanket." (The old man did come to church faithfully after that.)

Just about that time the runner came with the syringe. Of course we also prayed for both babies as well as giving them injections. Tubabufa's baby got well and so did Michele.

BUILDING

Although it took nearly a year from the time the first papers were processed until we obtained the land for the mission station, Mason had great faith that it would happen. He decided on wooden structures for the buildings that would be needed, and he began to make preparations. There was plenty of timber in the jungle but there were no sawmills in the area. We would have to make the boards by hand, a slow and tedious task. After extensively exploring the jungle within a few miles of Hageri, he found several stands of timber that would be suitable for the necessary wood. He found a pit saw—a narrow, two-handled saw used to cut planks—and two natives who had worked for the government and knew how to operate it. These men also helped him train other teams to do this work.

To set up the pit saw operation, we dug a deep trench about twelve feet long. After the tree was felled, we pulled it into position over the trench. The cutting teeth of the saw were set in only one direction, the stroke of the man standing in the bottom of the trench as he pulled the saw down. This was strenuous work. After the planks were cut, they then had to be carried the distance to the mission, sometimes one by one over trails so narrow it was necessary to walk single file to the house where they were placed on piles that were accumulating there. The green lumber had to dry out at least three months before it was fit to be used. We continued to cut, carry, and pile up planks, as we awaited our approval to build.

The native men were used to spending their days as they pleased—unless they were involved in a tribal war or needed to go hunting for birds or pigs or renew their arsenal of arrows. A definite work schedule was a foreign idea to them. Sometimes when Mason came to check the pit saw operation, he found that the men had forgotten all about their task and were engaged in idle pastimes. He told them he would only hire the men who would actually do the work, and only after they did the work would he pay them. This was a totally new concept in living for them. Slowly their attitude toward work changed as their lives were influenced by our examples.

AGRICULTURE

A New Guinea native woman already knew the discipline of a daily schedule and the rigors of hard work. For centuries their culture rendered the woman the responsibility of providing the family with food. She tended the gardens, cared for the children, and looked after the chickens and pigs. Pigs, which were a treasured possession, were given the same care as the children and shared the same quarters. She began the responsibilities of her day as soon as the sun began to rise. After the family and animals were fed and cared for, she tended the garden. The only tool she had for gardening was a sharp stick, which she used to make the holes in the ground when planting. She pulled the weeds by hand. At the end of the day she would settle down with the children and pigs, all snuggled together on the dirt floor. They had no blankets, so the only warmth they had came from each other and the smoldering fire in the middle of the hut. The men and older boys lived in their special communal men's house apart from the other members of the family.

We found that the people of the Dunantina Valley had existed for centuries on a very inadequate diet. *Kaukau*, which might be a distant cousin of the white sweet potato, was their staple food. They ate it morning, noon, and night. They also had a kind of cabbage and one or two other vegetables. The wild pig, the largest mammal native to New Guinea, supplied most of their meat, augmented with rats, snakes, beetles, and birds. Sometimes they would go for weeks without meat. Meat was used mostly for weddings, funerals, or special occasions. It would be cooked in a hole in the ground full of hot rocks, covered with banana leaves and dirt. A bamboo pole was inserted down the middle to pour water onto the hot rocks to create steam. This way of cooking is called a *mumu*.

One of the first things Mason did was plant a large garden to supply our family with food. It also served to introduce new vegetables to the natives. The Australian government agreed to supply them with seeds, so soon many of the native gardens were producing a nice variety of new foods. They also learned to grow many different types of sweet potato—white, purple, yellow, etc.—they are all tasty. We also provided them with better breed of pig, which improved their meat supply. They welcomed the new foods we introduced. Gradually their lifestyle started to change.

Teaching

Although it would be two years before our official day school would begin operation, we were teaching from the time we arrived at our little bush house. We taught the Word of God in services at the mission station and in villages, we taught hygiene and better ways of staying healthy. We taught the natives commerce by trading with them in the trade store. And we taught them various skills in many areas. But probably more importantly, from the first time the natives saw us, we taught them by the way we lived and loved and forgave and cared for and interacted with one another. And they were teaching us what it meant to be true "spiritual" missionaries.

Teaching the Word of God to the natives was at times very interesting. Their limited exposure to anything except the narrow culture in which their people had lived for centuries made communicating certain concepts of the Bible a puzzle and a challenge. The following redemptive analogy is one example of an innovative insight given to Mason by the Holy Spirit to teach a concept of Scripture.

My pigs know my voice and follow me

Mason had been going to different villages surrounding Hageri to tell the people about Jesus. Some of them were about eight hours away. So one day was spent walking there, he would stay over that night and some of the next day, and then he would come home. He had to be alert to the time for close to the equator, there is very little to alert that the sun is setting and rising—it is almost the same year-round. It would get dark and become daylight quickly—often without much twilight.

Typical Eastern Highlands village

On one of these trips, Mason had walked a long way across many rivers and streams into a village. He got there about four o'clock in the afternoon. He arrived when all the men were squatting on the side of a hill in the village. They were very thrilled to see him coming. He sat down with them. It was pretty warm, and he had just walked for hours. So, he took off his boots to rest his feet and removed his socks so they could air. That was the first time that they had ever seen his feet. They had seen him before, but because of being in the sun all the time his skin was tanned dark brown, almost as brown as they were. They even wondered why they called him the white man. But when he took his boots and socks off and they saw his white feet, a cry went up and they started pointing, just like children. All of the men came running over to see his super white feet—he was white after all!

Sitting there talking to the men, Mason notice that one of them said something to another who then stood up and got his bow and arrow. He went around beside the hut where we couldn't see him. We heard the twang of the bow as the arrow was fired and then heard the crying of a chicken. To Mason's surprise he came back with a chicken impaled on the end of his arrow. These chickens are not like our Rhode Island Reds. These are small, scrawny chickens with little colored feathers. They are as tough as nails to eat. The natives prepared a clay pot full of water. This clay pot is pointed on the bottom. They don't have wire to hang anything on, so they set up this pot with the pointed end buried in the ground and then they built a fire around it. This is how they boil the water. And while they were doing that, the women were preparing the evening meal by peeling *kaukau*.

Herds of pigs were milling around the village as they waited for their food—the peelings from the sweet potato. About twenty or thirty pigs composed a typical herd. One woman came out of her hut with a banana leaf full of sweet potato peelings for her pigs. She walked out the door and made a peculiar calling sound with her lips. A certain number of pigs, just her four, came out of that entire herd and went with her to be fed. She threw down the peelings to them and fed just those four. Mason looked out at the other huts, as we were in the middle of a lot of huts in this village. Another woman made the same peculiar sound and a certain number of pigs broke from the herd and came directly to her. The others pigs stayed in the herd and walked away. Only those certain pigs came to that certain lady's calling.

Mason thought that was very interesting. So he put his shoes on, and walked over to another hut where there were several pigs. He made the same peculiar sound he had heard the women make. He made it several times, but could not get any pigs to break from the herd and come to him. He could not get the attention of any pig no matter how many times he made the sound. It was as if they did not hear him. They paid no attention to his call at all. And yet another woman came out, made the same sound with the same tone, and a bunch of pigs broke from the herd and followed her.

Then it occurred to him that maybe he could use this example to illustrate a Bible story. The natives had never seen sheep, therefore it was very hard to explain to them the passage of scripture where Jesus said, "My sheep hear My voice, and I know them, and they follow Me" (John 10:27). Maybe he could explain this by using the pigs as an illustration. The pigs know their owners' voice and they follow them. They didn't know about sheep, but they did know that there was a certain sound that helped the pigs to follow their owner. They just might be able get the point about this scripture. They might be able to understand that Jesus knows each one of our voices just as the pigs know the voices of the women.

While Mason was contemplating this, one of men got up, took the chicken that was on the end of his arrow, went over to the clay pot of water that was being boiled, and stuck that chicken right into the boiling water. They didn't do anything to it; they didn't gut it or take off the feathers. That was going to be our meal for the night. When it was cooked, they just opened it up, pulled the meat out, and ate it. So did Mason; he was hungry.

There are a lot of very interesting stories like that from our travels in the jungles of New Guinea; this one was about the natives and their pigs. Oh yes, once Mason explained the verse in John to them relating it to pigs, they understood the meaning of the scripture.

Chapter 6
HAGERI, THE NEW MISSION STATION

Prepare your outside work, Make it fit for your-
self in the field; And afterward build your house.
—PROVERBS 24:27

DURING THE EARLY months at the bush house, so many
things pressed for immediate attention. We were holding
nine services a week and spending many hours ministering to the medical needs of the natives. We prayed daily for
the guidance of the Lord in setting up the proper priorities. It
was becoming urgent to make preparations for erecting permanent buildings for the mission station. The plan was to construct
the church building first. The crews were already working in the
jungle felling timber and sawing the planks we would use to
build. This lumber would be used for the buildings in the mission compound, including our permanent house.

FIRST THE HOUSE

Water was abundant in the Eastern Highlands. There were many
streams and rivers flowing from the mountains. During the
wet season, rain was a daily occurrence. Even in the dry season,
from mid-April to mid-October, it seldom went a week without
raining at least once. The pit-pit walls of our bush house kept
out the rain, and the grass roof was waterproof; but like all the
native huts, it was always damp. Twice already our little Michele

had pneumonia and she was only six months old. This was a great concern and the deciding factor for our building plans. A firm conviction took hold of Mason that we would build our house first, and then we would build the church.

But we had to wait for the government approval of our lease before the actual work of building could begin. One day we heard Ross's Land Rover coming down the road. He had great news from Port Moresby that our lease had been granted. This was wonderful news! The process of building began with fervor.

The Dunantina Valley and all the surrounding areas are mountainous. To find a spot on level ground is a rarity. Although it did run up the hill, we were grateful that our piece of land the Lord had chosen for us to build our missions station compound had comparatively level ground. But it was covered with kunai grass, so Mason hired several dozen men to pull the grass to prepare the new building site. As the tall kunai grass was removed, we were disappointed to discover that the land was very swampy, with deep muck and mire that did not dry out even in the dry season. So, before any building could be done, we had to drain the whole area. We hired the natives to help us first dig ditches five feet deep and eighteen or twenty inches wide. Then we filled the ditches with three feet of stone, which we got from the mountain river running from behind our mission station. We then covered the stones with two feet of soil. It took a dozen or more of these drainage ditches with connecting cross drains to do the job. Also, to help keep it dry, Mason planted many banana trees, as they absorb many gallons of water a day.

Though we would use the planks we were making from the jungle timber for the walls, we had to purchase flooring. By this time a sawmill had been established in Goroka where flooring could be cut; but, unfortunately, the truck sent to deliver it would not attempt our infamous Hageri Road. So all the flooring had to be hand carried that last five miles. When this part of the job was underway, the natives carrying the flooring were strung out for almost a mile down the trail that led up and down the hills to our land.

After everything needed for construction was accumulated, Mason found that he had to do much sawing and straightening, especially on the handmade planks. Often what was supposed to be a two-by-four turned out to be one-by-three or three-by-five. He soon found that his plan to let the natives help in the construction work had its limitations. They had no concept of measurements. If they did not saw straight on Mason's marked line, they would saw the board again and again, thus rendering many boards useless. Also, their hands were clumsy and awkward when they tried to handle the unfamiliar tools. They couldn't drive a straight nail. Nails were expensive, and they bent many before Mason realized their inability. With patience he straightened out the bent nails one by one. Thereafter he told the men to just hand him the nails and he would do the nailing. They had never seen nails before; and they found them fascinating, as the nails would magically hold the boards in place without vines. Mason began to notice his seventy-pound boxes of nails being depleted too quickly. After some observation, he found the natives were putting nails into their bushy hair and taking them home with them. Oh, for a scanner in those days!

Thus, the building progressed very slowly. Because of so many other pressing duties, it was hard for Mason to find time to work on the house. It was almost a year before he had the three bedroom house adequately finished for the family to move in. It was many more months before the interior was finished.

Our brand-new home made from pit sawed timber

THEN THE COMPOUND

After we moved into the house, we began the church building. By the time it was finished, we had already outgrown it; so we still had our larger services outside. The compound eventually included, in addition to our home and the church building, a school building, a trade store, a first aid station, a thousand gallon water storage tank, and miscellaneous other things. We also landscaped the whole mission compound. We planted 200 trees given us by the Australian government—klinki pines, eucalyptus, cashew nuts, oranges, grapefruit, and apples. We also planted an assortment of berries, vines, and flowering shrubs.

First church at Hageri Missions Station

Day school

About two years after arriving at Hageri, the school building was finished and we could open our much-anticipated day school. Several missionaries from Australia had come to teach and help with the mission work. Our school was a government regulated entity. Since there were so many dialects in the Eastern Highlands, and none of them were in writing, the New Guinea government required that the children attending school be taught in English. So our first priority was to teach the children an entirely new language, beginning with the ABCs. As soon as they were able to understand enough English to comprehend the subject matter, we began teaching them other subjects you would find in a regular school setting. We found that overall the natives picked up languages quite rapidly, many of them learning Pidgin also.

Like children in America, the abilities of the native children varied. Some did very well, considering their complete lack of educational background, while for others learning seemed very difficult. Their families eagerly awaited the day when their children came back to them with the ability to read. They were given Bibles from which they could read Bible stories to the family. For them it opened new and wonderful ideas and possibilities.

Although the native children were anxious to learn, they were still children. But it was necessary that discipline and order be maintained. We felt it unwise for any of the missionary teachers to punish the native children. So, when disciplinary issues arose at the school, we needed a native who could deal with them. One time when problems developed at the school with some of the younger boys, Sam was called to deal with the unruly youngsters. The patience and wisdom he showed in the emergency amazed us. When Sam was called to settle the disturbance, he reasoned with the boys before punishing them. The school boys stood in awe of Sam and rose to their feet in respect when he came into the classroom. Sam became a very important man—important to his people, important to us, and, most significantly, important to the Lord.

Sam takes a wife

One Sunday Sam asked to buy a knife he had seen in the trade store. "Sam, you know we don't open the store on Sunday," Mason told him. "Next week you can purchase the knife." "But, Master, you do not understand. I need the knife today!" he insisted. And then the story came out. Sam had found a girl he wanted to make his wife. He wanted to give her a gift. He did not want to wait until next week to give the knife. In his thinking, this was a momentous occasion and he wished to settle the matter with expediency. He felt that this knife would be the perfect gift, and he wanted to give it to her now—today! He would send her his knife with his best friend. If she kept it, then he knew she looked upon him with favor. If she returned the knife, well, then that would be the end of that.

Sam was invaluable to us; we let him have his way. How happy and proud he was to present his special girl the beautiful knife with the shining blade. She kept it! So far as we knew, Sam was the first man to choose his own bride. Sam was a tradition breaker and a man of unusual courage. It had long been the custom for the men of the village to live together in a sort of clubhouse or communal men's house, while each wife lived in her own small hut with her children and her pigs. But Sam and his wife, Zozabau, lived together in their new home we built on the mission compound.

Kiabe (Sam) with Mason and Virgene;
faithful interpreter and helper for twenty-three years

In the course of time, five children were born into their family: David, John, Christine, Miala, and Jimmy. Sam liked his name so much that he gave all of his kids Sam as their last name. Sam's eldest son, David Sam, became a pastor. He pastored several churches in different areas. He then became the pastor of a branch church in the city of Lae that had 1,200 people in attendance. We were so proud of him. Throughout the twenty-three years we were in Papua New Guinea and since, Sam has been a valued true and faithful friend to us.

Chapter 7
TABIAK AND SUNUPALA

Therefore, if anyone is in Christ, he is a
new creation; old things have passed away;
behold, all things have become new.
—2 CORINTHIANS 5:17

W E CONTINUED OUR ministry to the people, caring for their medical needs, treating them with kindness, and sharing with them the good news of Jesus Christ always ending with an invitation for them to receive Him. The witch doctors were afraid of this "Man" we spoke of who is more powerful than theirs; they had seen that power at work when they tried to put a curse on Kiabe but had failed. Their power was predicated on fear and superstition; so they were filling the people with bad news, frightening them with curses and ominous tales of what horrible things might happen to them if they responded to our words. There was a lot of questioning and considering going on in the villages. The natives pondered these new ideas we were presenting and considered whether there might actually be a better way of life. They were intently watching Kiabe and the changes that had come into his life. They saw good things. Nothing bad had happened to him. He was happy. But centuries of fear still held them back. They hesitated to try this new way of which we spoke.

Tabiak, Chosen by God

It was a Sunday morning and a large crowd had gathered. As always, the people listened attentively to the message Mason gave that was interpreted into their own language by one of them, Kiabe. As was our custom after each service, a call to receive Jesus was given. This time one man came forward. He stood before us in his native dress—bark loin cloth, feathers in his matted greasy hair, shells and bones piercing his ears and nose and hanging around his neck, with his man-killing arrows and bow clutched in his hands. He prayed to receive Jesus. This man was Tabiak. After our interpreter, Sam (Kiabe), he was our first convert at Hageri.

About two days later Tabiak came to the mission station. He wanted something, but it took about five minutes for us to understand what he wanted. At last by using sign language, we understood that he wanted scissors and clothes and soap. The next morning as we looked out our windows at the people always gathered around our house, we saw nice looking man among the others. We thought he must be a visitor from somewhere else. We asked Sam if he knew who that man was. He told us it was Tabiak. What a transformation! He didn't look like the same person as he stood there clean and clothed. He had bathed and washed in the river. His hair had been cut, washed, and brushed out. He had clothes on. He was even talking differently. Everyone saw the change in Tabiak. People came to us and said, "He is a different man. He doesn't want to fight any more!"

We had not told Tabiak what to do or what not to do. But after he prayed to receive Jesus, God began to transform Tabiak and his life. The next Sunday Tabiak brought his wife. She came forward and gave her heart to the Lord. In spite of the warnings from the witch doctors of the bad things that might happen to them if they received the "Man" we were telling them of, the people began to consider this new way because they saw that the things that happened to Tabiak were good things. There was not one bad thing that happened to him. He had joy and peace—and he had stopped swearing over night. Such love filled him that he did not wish to fight his neighbors anymore. He broke his man-killing arrows over his knee. Although he was completely unschooled, he memorized Bible stories so he could repeat them to his people. In his life the old things truly did pass away and all things became new. Only the Spirit of God could bring about such a transformation.

Tabiak and Zabaruta's first baby

This is the story of our first miracle on the mission station at Hageri. In New Guinea all the huts of the village are for the women and the children and their pigs. There is one big communal men's house where the men and the older boys all live together. Couples do not live together as husband and wife. Tabiak was the only one in his village who wished to take on a new lifestyle and live with his wife. The people of his village were upset. "Tabiak, you can't live like this among us. You don't fit any more. The life you now want to live is so different," they told him. Because of the joy and satisfaction that came to Tabiak as a believer, he was ready to lay aside his old ways. He was a man of great courage for he had stepped forward to try Christianity. "All right, I don't want to live among you if I have to go where you go and do what you do," Tabiak responded. "I have found the better way of life. I will move."

So Tabiak decided he wanted to come and live with his wife, Zabaruta, at the mission station. But the government would not allow anyone to build on the station except mission personnel, so we had to refuse Tabiak's request to build a home there.

Undaunted, he did what he determined to be the next best thing and built his house just outside the fence surrounding the mission compound. He and his wife came to the mission station to their new home and new lifestyle.

Sometime later Tabiak came to Mason with a bunch of sticks in his hands, what the natives use for counting. They don't have a calendar. They collect a stick for each full moon that goes by. They only have two words for counting— *magoki* and *taragi*— meaning one and two. We always tried to estimate how old they were by their health or their teeth or what they remembered of big events that happened in the past. Tabiak said, "It has been many years since we have been married, and we would like for you to give my wife a shot of penicillin. We would like to have a child now." (We estimated that it had been about six years that they had been married and had not yet had a child.) We were giving penicillin to those people who had terrible sores and sicknesses, and it helped them tremendously. So, Tabiak thought that it was a very powerful drug so it would help Zabaruta have a child.

Mason responded, "Tabiak, your wife does not need a shot of penicillin because that would not help her to have a child. But there is a God in heaven who answers prayer. And several times in the Bible, God has given a child to women who were unable to bear children. So we are going to pray for her and believe that God is going to give her a child." So Tabiak brought his wife and they knelt while Mason prayed, "Lord, bless this family who were so brave to step out when no one else would. They have forsaken the old ways and are serving You now. So just bless this home and give them a child." Tabiak rose from his knees and went away thanking the Lord. Nine months later a baby girl was born into that home. They brought the child down to our house and asked Virgene to name her. She named her Rebecca. That was the first miracle we had! And that miracle caused people to believe and have faith in the fact that God does hear and answer prayer, even for the impossible. What is impossible with man is made possible with God!

Tabiak's powerful prayer

Tabiak built his house beside the mission station at Hageri so that he could be close to the church. It was a common tradition that the men would often help clear large patches of rocky and weed-infested land so that their women could do the work of planting the sweet potato and other vegetables to grow a garden. Tabiak was clearing a large piece of land with an abundance of tall, dry, kunai grass. Kunai is about waist high when you walk through it. It grows quite tall in the wet season and becomes very dry tinder in the dry season. Tabiak was clearing this large piece of land by starting a fire in the middle of the property. This was the only way they knew how to clear the kunai grass and the other weeds, bugs, sticks, bushes, and worms that would often destroy a garden.

Unexpectedly, the wind came up, and it quickly blew sparks from his fire in the middle of his garden over to another area of dry grass. It quickly became an uncontrollable fire, and the flames started spreading through quite a large area outside of our property. Flames were spreading quickly in all different directions. They were lighting up the entire mountainside. Tabiak noticed that the flames were headed right into a village with many huts. Tabiak did not know what to do.

But he remembered that he had received Jesus Christ into his heart. His heart reminded him of Mason telling him that you can ask anything in Jesus' name and He will do it (John

14:13–14). And so Tabiak knelt down right there in his garden
and he prayed, "Lord Jesus, please stop this fire so that it does
not do any more destruction and does not hurt anybody or burn
up any huts; because," he went on, "You know that I'm innocent.
I did not mean to do this but the wind caused it to catch fire." So
he prayed, and he looked up and immediately saw the fire beginning to just die out. The huge flames literally stopped burning
and disintegrated.

He came running down to the mission station and said excitedly, "Matrapa, Matrapa, come and see! Come and see! Come!
Come and look!" Mason hurriedly followed him up the road
to where his property was and where they had planned to put
their garden. Together we walked along the clear edge of where
the grass had burned the four-foot tall kunai grass and had just
stopped. It was as if someone had doused the fire with water in
a straight line.

This is the promise of God. A believer can ask anything in
His name and He will do it if we can believe (John 14:14). Tabiak
had become a believer, and he believed in the Word of God. He
asked for the fire to cease, and he saw it stop. Stopping that fire
saved a lot of people. Stopping that fire saved many villages and
their belongings. Thank God for the power of prayer!

Tabiak became one of our strong leaders and helped us in the
ministry and helped many others on the station. The natives were
free to help us as they wanted to—they had no other employment or job to speak of. Their sole function was to plant and
harvest their gardens and raise their pigs. They would cultivate
their gardens, tend to their coffee plants, and pursue numerous
agricultural aspects of mountain life. They would often give us
the fruits from many of their plants. They would plant a passion fruit seed, build a six-stick fence around it, and cultivate it

to produce fruit. The soil there was very fertile. They would give us so much produce that we would take it to Goroka, sell it, and make some extra money to cover our gas expenses.

In the years that have passed since then, two more children were born to Tabiak and his wife. They have been faithful Christians through the years. Tabiak served as pastor of the main station church, and has done a wonderful job for the Lord. Rebecca grew up and had children; she named one of her children after our daughter Stephanie. We saw Tabiak at our fiftieth anniversary of the Foursquare work in Papua New Guinea in 2006. He is doing well and still loves the Lord.

SUNUPALA, A MATTER OF FIRST IMPORTANCE

"I wonder if Sunupala will be saved," Virgene pondered the Sunday morning of our first church service. She was reflecting on how frightened she and the children were at their initial meeting on Hageri Road. He and his hunting party were the first natives we had encountered as we were moving to the area.

The near naked savages, heavily armed with their bows strung and arrows in hand, gathered on the hillside near our little bush house. It had been only a short while since these men had seen our strange family settle in beside the Dunantina River. We had invited Chief Sunupala and the people of his village of Kalikalina to come to hear a message. Along with the frightening looking men, the women also came bringing their children and their pigs. A small pig was carried in their arms like a child; but if the pig was larger, they led it by a vine rope tied to one leg. Every woman had her *bilum*, a sort of string bag in which she carried her baby or other important possessions.

On this day adults and children were all on equal ground, coming to hear something new from these interesting white strangers. Besides Sam, our interpreter, we used pictures and visual aids to help bridge the gap in language. But it was difficult to communicate the concept of a God of love to these people who had never known tenderness. Their lives had been suffused with fear, hate, and superstition, all promoted by the witch doctor. These evil thoughts seemed to shackle their minds and hinder any notion that change might be possible. But in spite of all this, God gave us favor with Sunupala and his people. As a gesture of friendliness, they brought *kaukau* from their gardens to share with us.

Our lives may have spoken more clearly to them of what we were trying to tell them with words. Each morning when we lifted the shutters covering our glassless windows in the kitchen and dining room of our little bush home, the curious natives pressed close to see what was going on inside the house. It was a strange yet astonishing sight to see us bow our heads for grace and see the kindness and politeness and love we showed to each other as our food was served. How amazing to see a table set with dishes, knives, forks, and spoons and with an individual service for each person. They might have one clay pot or wooden bowl with everyone clambering for their portion at mealtime. Like goldfish in a bowl, we were under constant observation.

Sunday after Sunday the people gathered, and Sunday after Sunday Mason gave them the simple gospel message. The people had been driven by fear for centuries; it was difficult to comprehend a God of love. And yet they were drawn to the message of John 3:16: "God so loved the world, that He gave His only begotten Son, that whoever believes in him should not perish but have everlasting life." They asked to hear it over and over again. Sunupala would say, "It is too good to be true. But tell it all over again!" And we did; we repeated the wonderful story of Jesus and His great love for all mankind over and over again.

One day Chief Sunupala came to Mason, "Sunday is not enough. Will you tell my people this message more often?" In spite of our busy schedule, we held nine services each week. We continued to minister to their physical needs also, devoting several hours a day to the medical work. We were also ministering to their economic needs by introducing them to new vegetables and better gardening methods. We set up a trade store in an effort to expose them to some of the ways of the outside world. They would bring their surplus vegetables and would trade them for salt or some other item. One night, long after the service was ended and the people had returned to their homes, we lay in the darkness of our bush home. Mason turned to Virgene and said, "I believe God is going to give us Sunupala."

Sunupala becomes a Christian

Although Sunupala and the people of his village were among the first to attend Sunday services, it was several months before he decided to embrace a new way. The witch doctors and the fear they ruled by had such control over the minds and thoughts of the people, that the thought of anyone thinking for himself was a totally novel idea. New concepts had to be repeated over and over. Our words were strange, and the challenge of change they brought was disturbing.

Sunupala listened, marveled, and considered. He insisted that all the people of Kalikalina village attend the church services and hear the message of the missionary. But whenever invited to make a decision to receive Jesus, he would shake his head and say, "I must hear more." One day Sunupala surrendered with his whole heart. He encouraged the people of his village to follow his example, and they did. Every one of the people in his village came forward to receive Jesus as Savior.

Chief Sunupala and wife with child in new attire ready for baptism

Sunupala continued to request to hear the Bible stories over and over again. He memorized them and then went to neighboring villages share the amazing story of the Savior who died on the cross for them. Sunupala, the frightening looking chief who had lived in fear and hatred, became a new man, a new creature in Christ and a missionary to many people in hidden and forgotten valleys. Only the power of God can transform the hearts of men.

Chapter 8
"MAKE DISCIPLES"

*Go therefore and make disciples of all the nations,
baptizing them in the name of the Father and of the
Son and of the Holy Spirit, teaching them to observe
all things that I have commanded you; and lo, I
am with you always, even to the end of the age.*
—MATTHEW 28:19–20

W E VENTURED INTO the surrounding areas around Hageri and managed to start works in nine different villages—all in opposite directions from Hageri. Some were five hours away, others three hours, and some even farther. Mason would spend most nights sharing Bible stories and training and teaching others. Many people were receiving Jesus as their Savior and the work was growing. Mason soon realized it was becoming difficult to visit all these surrounding villages in addition to the many other needs in establishing and maintaining the main mission station. And so we began to pray, "Father, we need help to come." As the scripture says, "Therefore pray the Lord of the harvest to send out laborers into His harvest" (Matt. 9:38). And even on the hardest day, we began to pray, "Lord, send us laborers to help in this great harvest that we have in Papua New Guinea." And He did in many different ways.

NINE MEN

One day, soon after that prayer, a knock came on our door. Mason opened the door to find nine men standing there. Just to say that there were nine men standing there needs to be clarified a little bit. These nine men, with bows and arrows in hand, were dressed in warrior feather headdresses, had pig tusk bones through their noses, and carried stone axes hung from grass woven belts around their waists.

Tribal warrior

They said, "May we help you?" Mason replied, "No, no thank you." They insisted, "We have come to help you." Mason thought to himself, "Well, I have plenty of natives around here to help me." Curious, he asked, "In what way do you want to help me?"

They responded, "We want to help you in the nine different places where you have been going." "How did they know exactly the nine places I had been going?" Mason pondered. Then he began to look more closely at these men. Their faces were familiar. Each man was from one of the nine different places, places miles apart and separated by mountains and rivers. So Mason thought, "This really must be God. God has sent these nine men here. But what am I going to do with them? They cannot read or write. They do not have a Bible."

Mason was young, twenty-eight years old, and this was all new to him. We were taught in Bible school that to be a pastor you need to know the Bible, you need to be formally trained, and you must have pastoral training. So, as Mason looked at these primitive men, he thought, "Thanks, but no thanks." And then the Holy Spirit spoke to his heart, "What have you been praying about lately?" He responded to the Holy Spirit from his heart, "Well, I have been asking for laborers to come and help me with this overwhelming work of the ministry." When we prayed we were thinking of qualified and trained laborers from Australia or America. We had no thought of any other source from which we might receive help. And the Lord spoke again, "You have nine men standing before you! What's your problem?"

As the Lord directed him to Matthew 28:20, "Teaching them to observe all things that I have commanded you," Mason realized that he was to teach them. So the Lord was showing him that not only was it a miracle that these men came from these nine different places at the same time, but that it was the Holy Spirit that guided them and brought them to him. These men were saved. They were filled with the Holy Spirit. And these are the two things they really needed in order to do the work of the ministry.

So Mason opened the door wide and invited them in. As these men came in, he got nine chairs and lined them up for them to sit on so he could talk with them. Although he had been in the bush for awhile, he was still learning. The men looked at the chairs and walked around each one. Finally, one of the braver men decided he would try the chair. So he stepped up onto the seat of the chair with his feet and squatted down in it. And when Mason saw the other men start to do the same, he decided to move the chairs away. He realized immediately that they had never sat in a chair because they didn't have chairs. In fact, they didn't often sit on anything—they squatted on the ground. So Mason squatted with them and began to tell them the stories about Jesus—the works that Jesus did, the people that Jesus healed, the journeys that Jesus took, the miracles that He performed. They were so happy to hear all these stories of Jesus.

The people of New Guinea had no clocks or calendars. They did not have a concept of time as we know time; they didn't have any sense of time lapse or history at all. The good part about that was, when they heard the stories about Jesus, they were to them as though they had happened just last night! Also, the people of Papua New Guinea developed a supposition as they began to come to and serve the Lord; that supposition was that if He ever did it for anyone whenever, He would do it for them anytime.

So they took these stories Mason told them and they went back to their villages, promising that they would come see him again. He also continued to go to the villages every two weeks to meet them there and train them. The men returned to the main mission station weekly to receive more stories and training. Mason would always have them repeat to him the stories that they had heard the week before so he could be certain they were getting them right.

One week one of them came in and said, "Last week you told me how Jesus healed the blind man." Mason responded, "Yes, can you repeat it to me?" And he said "Oh yes, I can repeat it to you. Not only that, I have a blind man in my village. I couldn't wait to get home to pray for him! When I got to my village, I got all the people together and I told them the story. Then I prayed for the blind man and then Jesus opened his eyes! He can see!" Mason began to praise the Lord. How He was using these men! Two weeks later another man said, "Last week you told us how Jesus healed the crippled man. I have a crippled man in my village. I was anxious to get home and tell my people the story of how Jesus healed a crippled man. After I told the story, I prayed for this crippled man and Jesus healed him. He's walking today!" Mason thought, "I had disqualified these men because they had no formal Bible training and no academic setting in which to learn. Yet God had chosen them as leaders who would begin the work of sincerely pastoring their own people in Papua New Guinea."

About a month after this happened, one of the men told Mason about the last time he had gone home to his village. He said, "The last time I was here, as I was going home and came around the bend in the trail, I saw a lady from another village hanging dead from a tree. And I was so disappointed because I knew that she had never heard about Jesus. There was no one to tell her but me." He continued, "I also knew that the enemy is always seeking who he can devour. He knew I was coming that way, so he got ahead of me and somehow convinced this woman to take her life so that she would not be able to hear the story of Jesus. I was mad at the devil! So I climbed that tree, I cut the rope vine, and I carried her down. I laid her on the ground, and I said, 'Now, Lord Jesus, put life back into this woman so I can talk to her and let her have a chance to hear about You so she can make a decision about what she wants to do in life.' So I asked the Lord Jesus to put life into her. She immediately stood up on her feet! And then I explained to her how I understood that we have an enemy, the devil, that is out to kill and destroy and that he had knowledge of me coming that way that day. I told her, 'So he had somehow incited you to take your life. But Jesus loves you. He loves you so much that He has put life back into you again and He sent me this particular way to go home today so that I might find you on this trail and that I might tell you about His great love for you. Now you have a choice. Do you want to receive Jesus into your heart and serve Him and love Him, or do you want to serve the enemy that took your life?'" That woman opened up her heart and received Jesus Christ and is living for the Lord today. And after that, a church was planted there and a new work was started in that village.

Many of our works were started through miracles that happened amongst the people in that particular area. Praise the Lord! Those first nine men multiplied into many, many more men serving the Lord and receiving the baptism of the Holy Spirit. We called them "Leader Boys." We made sure that they received training and discipleship. We had a policy that every pastor who was pastoring a church must select two others that he was to disciple. There was always someone training new disciples, always someone to help the pastor, and always someone to take over when the pastor had to travel or be gone for any reason. "The Lord gave the word; Great was the company of those who proclaimed it" (Ps. 68:11).

We praise the Lord for those nine men who were obedient to the voice of the Holy Spirit as He spoke to their hearts and directed them to Hageri to become the first pastors of their village. By the way, the Lord later sent many workers from Australia, New Zealand, and America to help in the work of Papua New Guinea.

Go Tell It on the Mountain

This story is about an elder from the church in Hageri who went to Mount Sunabiga. One Sunday morning after the second service, everyone was standing around fellowshipping when the Lord spoke to this elder. The Lord said, "I want you to go up Mount Sunabiga and tell these people about Me because they have not come down to the church since the mission has been here. So you must go up to them." But the elder responded, "Well, I'm not a minister. I'm not a pastor. I can't read or write. I don't have a Bible. How can I go tell them?" And the Lord spoke to his heart again and told him, "Just tell them what you heard the missionary say this morning." So the elder thought, "Well, I can go and tell them what I heard the missionary say this morning in church because it was very good."

So he started out climbing that steep mountain. He arrived at the village on Mount Sunabiga. He told the people that he was there to bring a good message to them—a message that would help them; a message that would make a better life for them. So they gathered around and they listened to the message that the elder had to tell them.

When he finished he thought, "What will I do now?" He pondered for a moment, "Well, Matrapa would always give an invitation for them to receive the Lord Jesus into their hearts and be saved. So I can do that too." So he invited everyone who wanted to receive the Lord to come kneel down on the ground and he would pray and help them to open their hearts to receive the Lord Jesus Christ into their lives. Quite a number of people came forward. And they all received Jesus Christ as their Savior. He was so happy.

Then he thought, "Well, Mr. Hughes always prays for people to be healed after the service, so maybe I should do that too." So he told the people, "If anybody has sick people in your hut, bring them and we will pray that God will heal them." Everybody began to run here and there and everywhere. They came back carrying people with all kinds of ailments. There were men and women and children that needed healing. There were so many sick that he lined them up. Then he went down the line praying for all of them and laying his hands on all of them, just as he had seen Mason do so many times before. And he found that God was answering his prayers just like He answered Matrapa's prayers.

When he came almost to the end of the line, there was a man standing there holding a little boy about four years old in his arms. The elder looked at him and said, "What is wrong with this little boy?" The father responded, "You told us to go and get all the sick people and bring them and you would pray for them and the God that you have been talking about will heal them. My little boy died yesterday. Today we were going to have a ceremonial burial and do a funeral, but you said to bring anybody sick. I thought he must really be sick, so I brought him to you that you might pray for him." The elder was astounded. He didn't know what to do. He had never done anything like that before. "But," he thought, "I will go ahead and do what the Lord has told me to do. He told me to come here, so He must want me to do this." So he prayed for the little boy. The Lord spoke to him, "Before the sun goes down I will put life back into that little boy. You tell the father that." So he looked up at the father and he said, "Before the sun goes down the Lord will put life back into that little boy."

So everybody went on their way back to their huts to get some *kaukau* to eat. All the men gathered around the hill. The elder thought, "I'm going to stay here. I want to see when it happens." (When this elder was telling this part of the story, Mason thought, "That *is* really brave. I might have been getting off that mountain, just in case.") But the elder had faith to believe that what God said He would do, He would do. So he sat down with the rest of the men. Before the sun went over the mountaintop—just before it began to set—they were all astonished. They heard a loud cry. They looked up and here came the very same little boy walking out of the hut where they had placed his dead body. He was crying out for something to eat, so they got a sweet potato and began to feed him. God was, once again, true to His Word. He had put life back into that little boy from the prayer of this elder.

So that was a rare encouragement to these villagers. They often thought that only the missionary had power to break the power of sickness or a binding curse. But they discovered that God would answer their prayers too if they would just pray in faith and believe. That was a wonderful experience for the church at Hageri. The people on Mount Sunabiga asked us to send a pastor there as a result of this miracle. A church service was started on Mount Sunabiga. They would gather together regularly on Sunday mornings and nights. They even started gathering together every night when they had a leader to conduct services. They would pray and the leader would tell the stories that he had learned from us.

Up to that point all the pastors and leaders would come into the mission station once a week. They couldn't read or write, so they would memorize the story Mason told them and then they would go back to their people and tell them that story. It was really a wonderful thing that happened there. God decided He would speed up and expand the process a bit by sending an elder to Mount Sunabiga. We hadn't yet thought to do that. So, praise the Lord that He is on His throne and He will build his church. As he said, "I will build My church, and the gates of Hades shall not prevail against it" (Matt. 16:18). Amen.

The Church That Was Built with a Handful of Salt

Just as he closed one Sunday morning service at the mission station in Hageri, Mason noted the arrival of a stranger, and sent Sam to speak to the man. "A handful of salt—just a handful of salt, that's all he wants," said Sam as he returned to report to Mason. "You know the trade store is never open on Sunday, Sam. Tell him to come back tomorrow and we will be glad to let him have some salt." Again Sam spoke with the man. He gave Mason the gist of the conversation. "This is Tamazio, a great chief from a distant village. You have never visited his people. He has never been here to the mission station before. But he has heard about the salt which you have given our people. Everyone tells him that it gives a wonderful taste to food, especially pig meat. Now he is giving a great feast in his village. As a special treat, he has promised to get salt for his guests." "Too bad he didn't come yesterday when the trade store was open," Mason replied. "But tell him to come back tomorrow, and we will let him have all he needs. Explain to him that the store is open six days a week, but that Sunday is a day of worship. The store is not open today for that reason." Again there was much talk in the native dialect and Mason watched as Sam tried to explain to the chief. He could see that Tamazio was insisting with much vehemence. "Master," said Sam. "Tamazio does not want to wait until tomorrow for the salt. He wants it now. He has already killed several pigs in preparation for the feast. His guests have already arrived, and he has promised to have salt for them when he returns. He wants salt now."

Mason had never been faced with a decision just like this, for the natives among whom he worked did not question his word. When he said the store would be closed on Sunday, they offered no strong protest. Sometimes they forgot and asked for something, but when he said a firm, "No," they did not argue. Sunday was a busy day for him, and if he humored one, others would think of things they wanted too. But most important of all, he wished to teach them to respect Sunday as a day of worship.

Before we came, these people had never tasted salt; but once they tasted it, they were wild about it and considered it a great luxury. They had no medium of exchange; so in order to introduce them to some of the customs of the outside world, we set up a native trade store. When a native had more *kaukau* or other vegetables than he needed for his own family, he brought it to us and received salt in exchange. When we needed firewood, we paid for it with salt. News of this wonderful delicacy spread from tribe to tribe, and far over the mountains into many a hidden valley where we had never set foot. So the people came from far and near to get salt.

"Tell Tamazio to come back tomorrow and we will be glad to let him have what he wants," Mason said with finality. When Sam delivered the message, Tamazio just stood there. It seemed that he could not conceive of anyone refusing to grant his wish. A chief expects everyone to give him what he wants—but the missionary had refused him. Finally he dropped his head in disappointment. Slowly and sadly he turned to retrace his steps back down the trail. As they watched his retreating figure, the natives began to talk in great excitement, gesticulating wildly. Realizing there was a vast chasm separating the culture of these people from his own and desiring to build a bridge of friendship, Mason asked Sam and others what he should do. "Master, can't you let him have the salt this one time?" they pleaded. "Tamazio has never heard the gospel. He does not know about Sunday. Tamazio is a great chief! If we make him angry, maybe he never comes again!"

The voice of the Lord spoke to Mason's heart: "Listen to these counselors." "Tamazio!" he called, "Come back. Let us talk more. I have a plan." Tamazio retraced his steps and stood waiting while Mason explained the plan to Sam. "Tell him if he will promise to bring his people to church next Sunday, I will give him all the salt he wants today." Sam delivered the message. Tamazio stood silent. Everyone waited in suspense as several minutes passed while Tamazio thought the proposition over carefully. At last he raised his head. "It is agreed. You give me the salt today; I bring my people next Sunday." Quickly the salt was provided, and Tamazio went back to his people with joy.

The following week was a very busy time at the mission station, and with the press and rush of other activities, the incident was forgotten. Sunday morning dawned bright and clear. Very early we heard a great commotion up on the mountain just back of the mission station. "Sam, come here!" Mason called. "What's going on up there on the mountain?" As they watched, a long line of people walking single file came down the narrow trail winding back and forth on the steep mountainside. As the leaders approached the mission station, there was still a long line that stretched back up the mountain. "Perhaps it is a funeral or a wedding or a sing-sing [a gathering where they dance and sing]. They are just passing through on their way to another village," they mused. By this time the leader had reached the fork in the trail. But instead of going on down the valley as they expected, he turned into the mission compound, and the others followed. "It's Tamazio!" Sam cried. "It's Tamazio and his people. Tamazio has kept his word! He has brought his people just as he promised last Sunday when you gave him that handful of salt!"

We could scarcely believe our eyes, but we went ahead with the service just as usual. The sermon that morning was a simple message, telling the story of a God of love who sent His only Son to redeem sinful men. At the close, when the call was given inviting all who wished to accept Jesus as Lord and Master to come forward, Tamazio and thirty-five of the leaders of his tribe answered the call by rising and going forward. It was all done quietly. An onlooker might have wondered if these natives understood what they were doing. But the change that came to Tamazio's village and into the lives of those people was unbelievable. And they built a church—a church that today is one of the strongest in that area—a church that was built with a handful of salt.

Tamazio gave up his chieftainship, because he went no more out to war. The desire to fight and kill was gone from his heart. He spent his time learning Bible stories that he could tell his people. After a period of preparation and training, Tamazio became the pastor of one of the largest churches of that area— the flourishing church at Zanofi.

BAIESO

This story is about Baieso. Baieso was an assistant chief. He was a very important man. He came from his village, Gotomi, to visit us. He walked the entire six-hour distance. There were no horses, no bicycles, or any type of motorized transport. So he walked from his village to Hageri just to see the missionaries and to see how we lived. We lived much differently than they did. They just lived in a hut with a dirt floor and a fire burning in the center. They cooked their sweet potatoes in the fire and peeled it off bit by bit, ate it, then threw away the peelings to their pigs. They didn't have dishes to wash. They didn't have pots and pans to clean up. They heard about the missionaries and how we cooked on the stove and used cooking pots and pans. We ate from a plate or a bowl with a fork and knife and spoon. So they all liked to come and look through the open shutters at what we were doing. It was very exciting to them.

So Baieso arrived at the station late in the afternoon. Mason met him and was showing him around and introducing him to everyone. He realized it was quite late and invited him to spend the night. "Tomorrow morning I have to go to Goroka and I'll be going right by the trail that will lead to your village. I'll drop you off at Lampo—that's where your trail begins." So the next day Mason put a few people in the front of the Jeep and put Baieso in the back. We started off down the road intending to drop him off at the trail that would lead him to his village. We could only drive about ten to fifteen miles per hour at the very most on these potholed, muddy, winding, gravelly dirt mountain roads.

Baieso steps off the Jeep

As we got close to where Baieso would get off at Lampo, Mason thought that Baieso might not recognize where he was, so he was preparing to stop and speak to him. As Mason looked in the rearview mirror, much to his amazement, he saw Baieso move towards the back and step out of the Jeep! Mason was driving about ten to fifteen miles per hour on a gravel dirt road and he just stepped out of the moving vehicle! He saw Baieso just tumbling and rolling along the road. Mason stopped the Jeep, ran back, and helped him stand to his feet. He took out his handkerchief and wiped away as much dirt and gravel as he could.

The New Guineans wore only a G-string bark loin cloth, with feathers on their heads and shells and pig tusks through their noses. They didn't have much covering their skin; a lot of skin is exposed. Mason noticed that Baieso didn't have too many bruises or scratches, but he did have some minor scrapes and bleeding. He wiped his head, as it did have lot of little scratches on it, and said, "Do you want me to take you with me to Goroka to see the doctor?" Baieso responded, "No, I don't need to go see a doctor." So Mason wrapped his handkerchief around his head and apologized, "Well, I'm sorry that I didn't tell you about not being able to step out of a moving vehicle." He had never been on anything moving before in his life. He didn't know that you couldn't just step off the Jeep onto the road. It was a hard experience for him to learn.

Seeing that he was alright, we said our good-byes and went on to Goroka. After concluding our business in Goroka, it was about 4 o'clock in the afternoon when we stopped at Lampo. Mason noticed that there were a lot more people in the village than normal. And as he walked deeper into the village, he noticed that one man had a white handkerchief on his head. He knew who it was because the natives didn't have any type of clothing at all. It was Baieso—the young man that had stepped off the Jeep that morning. So Mason went to him and said, "Baieso, didn't you go home?" "Oh yes," he said. "I went to my village. But I was thinking all the way to my village that I have never been treated so kindly. Instead of slapping me and cursing me, you were kind to me and you even gave me this." And he pointed to the handkerchief around his head. "And I thought I must come and hear the story that this man has to tell. So I got all of my people that I could at that time of day and I brought them here with me." He had about thirty people with him from his village who he managed to gather at that time of day. And they walked all the way from their village out to Lampo and were waiting for us to come back.

Mason began talking through an interpreter, telling them the story of Jesus, as they didn't know anything but their own language at that point in time. Baieso had been to the coast of New Guinea and he knew Pidgin but Mason still used an interpreter so all the people would understand what he was saying. He gave them the story of Jesus and His love and how God loves them and can help them. He explained how God sent Jesus to die for them that they might have everlasting life. He told them if they would believe in Him, the Bible says whoever calls upon the name of the Lord shall be saved. But first of all, they must believe. He spoke to them about the miracles of Jesus. There wasn't a lot of preaching done with the natives. It was more teaching, talking to them, telling them the story, and then sitting down and giving them an opportunity to talk among themselves about how they should respond. Sometimes they would say, "We will wait and hear some more." So we would come back another time.

But today when Mason asked if anybody wanted to receive this Jesus into their heart and receive newness of life and have their sins taken away, Baieso was the first to stand up. They always squat down close to the ground. He stood right up and put his hand behind him and made a motion to his people. Then thirty of his people that came with him got up and they all came forward. Mason led them in prayer that the Lord Jesus would come into each heart, forgive their sins, and make each a new creature. Each one repeated the words that he was saying through the interpreter. Jesus came into their hearts and they received Christ on that very day. Praise God for what God did that day! A little kindness to a man who mistakenly stepped off a moving Jeep; and now he and his village found the Lord Jesus Christ as their own personal Savior.

Baieso lived in the village of Gotomi which is about a six-hour walk for Mason; the natives walk it in much less time. You have to cross a big river in order to get to their village. So Baieso said, "How are we going to hear more? How are the rest of my people going to hear? You must come and bring this message to my people." Well, it was difficult to say no. We were already going to nine different places in addition to having our own services on the main station. That is a demanding week. It was extremely difficult to work in another village during the week. Mason said, "I can only come every other week. But I will definitely come and see you." What that meant was that he would be leaving the Jeep at the end of the road and walking for six hours, fording the river, crossing over the mountain, and walking through the neighboring valley to their village. There he would tell them the story about Jesus. It was a wonderful experience to walk back into that area, to go into a place where people had never heard and to be able to tell them the story of Jesus. To share with them that whosoever calls upon the name of the Lord shall be saved was a blessing. To tell them that they had only to believe in Him was a revelation to these villagers. And that was because of Baieso and his willingness to bring thirty of his people to hear the story at Lampo.

Baieso challenged by demon-possessed man

The Lord is always with us and the enemy cannot stand this. The enemy knew what had happened in Baieso's life. The enemy did not like losing ground. And it was typical of the enemy to arrange for a man who was possessed by demons to challenge new Christians. And indeed Baieso's belief in God was about to be challenged. As Baieso was walking down the narrow village trail, he noticed a man coming towards him. The village trails in the mountains are very narrow—just a tiny foot trodden path through dense jungle—and one would have to step off the trail to let another pass. This man had his stone ax lifted in the air—in an attack and kill ready position—and he demanded that Baieso bow down before him. The enemy always wants people to bow down before him to worship him. Baieso stopped, and he looked at the quickly approaching man.

He told us this story: "I prayed and I said, 'Papa God, help this man.' And the man just kept walking quickly towards me and coming right at me. And I prayed the second time, 'Papa God, help this man.' And it wasn't long until the man was within close striking range to me with his ax raised ready to strike as if to kill me. And for the third time I prayed, 'Papa God, help this man.' And as I prayed that prayer the third time, the man lowered his ax, fell on his knees, dropped his ax on the ground, and surrendered his heart to the Lord Jesus Christ." The man instantly felt a greater power than he had ever felt before.

Baieso was brave enough to trust wholeheartedly in God that he believed and stood his ground unafraid. So this man also came to the Lord Jesus Christ because Baieso boldly stood there and held his ground. Baieso put into practice 1 John 4:4 that says, "He who is in you is greater than he who is in the world." When Mason heard this story from Baieso, he told him "You know, Baieso, that's a strange prayer. I think I would have been praying, 'Lord, help *this* man,'" and Mason pointed to himself. And here is what Baieso replied. "That man needed help. I don't need help because I'm ready to meet the Lord." Mason thought, "What a wonderful thing to believe and understand that now you are a child of God, God will take care of you. Even in death you are rewarded with a place in heaven where you will be with Him forever and ever. It is those on earth that do not know Him that really need help." That is pretty good theology that Baieso had learned.

Chapter 9
INAGORI:
THE MAKING OF A MISSIONARY

I delight to do Your will, O my God, And
Your law is within my heart.
—PSALM 40:8

I NAGORI LIVED IN the village of Benaganofi. He had a cousin named Musoso who had been his playmate for years. But Musoso's family had moved from Benaganofi to the valley. Although Inagori was very lonely without Musoso, he was too shy to leave his village and travel into the valley to see him. After a few months Musoso walked up to Benaganofi to see Inagori and give him some exciting news. The boys were so very happy to see each other. Musoso told Inagori, "In the valley at Hageri there are missionary people who have come. They have children that are white! They have meetings and even a special meeting for boys and girls. Oh, Inagori, it is good! They told us a beautiful story about a Man called Jesus and a kind lady showed us some pictures. Come with me next Sunday."

Inagori was very interested in what Musoso was saying and he wanted to go but he had never seen a missionary before and that made him nervous. He inquired of Musoso, "Will they like me? Will they be angry with me?" Musoso assured him that they would be glad to have him come. So the next Sunday Inagori came to Hageri with Musoso.

INAGORI'S DECISION

This Sunday Mason told the story of God's Creation. Inagori was enthralled with the story. Then, as always, Mason told the story of Jesus and His love for mankind in dying on the cross and gave an invitation to all who were willing to receive Jesus. Inagori responded to the call and went to the front where he prayed with Mason with the help of Sam, the interpreter. God immediately began a great work in Inagori, and Mason knew he was different. Inagori knew the God who lived in heaven and brought the missionaries to tell him the story of Jesus now lived inside of him and had cleansed him and taken away his sin.

He asked Mason what he had poured on him while he was praying, as he felt like water was being poured on him. Since Mason hadn't poured anything, no doubt this was the anointing of the Holy Spirit. Inagori was a changed boy. Joy filled his heart for he had found a real purpose in life. Back in his village Inagori began thinking about the story of Jesus. Many questions came to him: "Where in New Guinea did Jesus die? Why haven't I heard of Him before? Where did He live? Was He from the coast? Why have I never seen Him?" Inagori's trip to Hageri was the farthest he had ever been from his village of Benaganofi. He knew very little of his country beyond his own mountain range. He thought all white people were born at the coastal towns of New Guinea. But now one thing he knew without a doubt was the story of Creation. And he knew the God who made it all—the food, the water, the trees, the fire, the sun, the rain, our bodies.

Inagori ran down the mountain early the next Sunday morning. This week Virgene had Sunday school for the children. She told the story of Jesus and the little children and how much He loves them. She shared the scripture where Jesus said, "Let the children come to me. Don't stop them for the kingdom of

Heaven belongs to those who are like these little children" (Matt. 19:14, NLT). Then she showed a picture of Jesus nailed to the cross. It gripped Inagori's heart to see His nail-pierced hands. He better understood the crucifixion and death of his beloved Savior. Then Virgene told the children that Jesus died not only to take their sins away but also to heal their bodies. If they prayed, God would heal them. Inagori began practicing this concept whenever he injured himself. The Lord was faithful to answer a little boy's prayers.

Not long after his salvation experience, Inagori told his family that he had decided to be baptized. He invited them all to go to Hageri with him the next week to the baptism. Begalanabi, his father, told him of something that had happened years before when Inagori was a baby. They had walked to another mission at a nearby village to hear a native pastor tell about Jesus. After they had gone many times to these meetings, Begalanabi wanted to be baptized. Unfortunately, the pastor told him that he didn't "pass the test." He was so disappointed and discouraged that he never went back and wasn't interested in going to church with Inagori.

In spite of those past hurts, all of little Inagori's family and many of his village were present when he was baptized in the Dunantina River at Hageri. The service was wonderful. All the people who came from the village of Benaganofi heard the story of Jesus. They made decisions to receive Jesus. The next week they brought their friends, and spouses and children. Many were saved through this little boy's heart for God and obedience to His word. He was already beginning to be a missionary.

Inagori speaks of this in his testimony, "When I was a little boy, after I had found Jesus as my Savior, I loved Him with all my heart. All I wanted to do was to work for Him by telling my people and others in neighboring villages about Jesus and how He died to save them. My constant prayer was: 'I want to be a missionary, Jesus. Please teach me Your Word so I can tell others about You.' I told my village people that I wanted to be a missionary, but they laughed at me. I told them that they mustn't smoke or say bad words when they were near me because I didn't want to hear them."

Inagori goes to school

The two young cousins, Inagori and Musoso, along with many others were among the first pupils enrolled in our day school. Inagori loved the school where he heard the Word of God every day. He worked diligently to hide it in his heart (Ps. 119:11). Not long after the school opened, Ian Van Zuilecom arrived and began an English-speaking Bible school for the children.

Later a special prayer meeting was organized for the school boys every Wednesday night. Although many of the boys didn't come because they didn't want to pray, Inagori attended along with his friend Metikau from Gotomi. For the very first time he heard people speaking in tongues. "When I heard people speaking in the heavenly language, I knew it was another blessing from the Lord. I wanted it, too," said Inagori. "I kept coming to the meetings, and I continued to pray that I might receive the Holy Spirit and speak in other tongues. One night only a few of my friends came to the prayer meeting. None of us had received the Holy Spirit. A missionary, Mrs. Pearson, rose to close in prayer, and she told us that God would fill us with the Holy Spirit now if we only believed. We began praying again, and I said, 'Jesus, I want to be a missionary to tell my people about You.' Then quickly, the Lord began to fill me with the Holy Spirit, changing my language. I began to sing in the Spirit, too, singing many new spiritual songs. I felt the power of God going through my body like rain coming down upon me. I was praising God with all my heart. I kept speaking in tongues for a very long time. When I went home to bed, I couldn't sleep. All night I thought about this wonderful new experience with God, my Father. Now I really understood that Jesus was in heaven and I knew He would hear and answer my every prayer, so I can work for Him."

After this baptism in the Holy Spirit, Inagori's hunger God's Word grew even stronger. He would ask his teachers to write scriptures on a piece of paper to help him memorize them. Then he could teach them to the other boys and the people in his village. He asked for a Bible of his very own so he could read and study it. By the time Inagori was only fourteen years old, he had already learned much of the Word of God. He told Mason he really wanted to work for the Lord and asked where he could go. Mason told him to begin at home and that later the Lord would lead and direct him to the place where he could best serve. Inagori took Mason's words to heart and began holding regular services in his own village of Benaganofi.

In only a few months we were able to tell Inagori that he and Metikau had been chosen to go to Australia for a year of schooling and Bible school training. "I knew it was the Lord's will for me to go to Australia in His service," said Inagori. "He saw my heart's desire and He answered my prayer. I wanted to go to Australia to work for the Lord, not for my own selfish gain. So I promised Jesus to work for Him. I knew that if I disobeyed, I would be like Jonah and would reap what I had sown."

The boys lived with missionaries Ray and Tryph Pearson in Australia. They attended school and had their own little service in the home together each day. They studied the Bible in great detail, along with the trials and triumphs of the Old and New

Testament characters. These studies helped the boys to grow and develop into more mature Christians.

Inagori's burden for his people back in New Guinea, especially those in his own village, became greater while he was in Australia. His people did not have a missionary who could help them each day. "I knew that some of them were still living in sin and they needed God's Word every day," said Inagori. "I prayed to the Lord and asked Him to help me to still be one of my people and not to change my ways so that I could help my New Guinea people. I was hungry to know more of Him and His Word. I was thankful that I could learn this in Australia. But I wanted to stay a New Guinean so that when I returned home, I could reach my people on the same level as they were."

The Lord was faithful to answer Inagori's prayers. He returned to Hageri to complete his basic schooling. He tells his own story: "In 1966 I graduated from our mission primary school at Hageri, and went into Goroka to attend the high school. Again, I didn't want to leave my people but told the Lord that I wanted to be a missionary in Goroka—I didn't want to work for the government. After school and on the weekends, I walked around the town witnessing to the people, visiting nearby villages, and preaching at every opportunity. I was very happy working for the Lord, telling these new people about Jesus."

Broader fields of service

While attending high school in Goroka, Inagori faithfully witnessed of Jesus Christ and His love. He led many of his school friends to Christ. Later some of these boys entered Bible school training and went to serve the Lord in the Western Highlands. One Sunday as Inagori was walking around the streets of Goroka, he went to the gaol (prison). He felt strongly impressed that he must go inside and tell the men of Jesus Christ. As he approached the gate, he prayed, "God, let me into this place." Just then a policeman came over and told him to come in. Inagori told the policeman that he wished to hold a service and tell prisoners about Jesus. The policeman thought that was a great idea and also wanted to hear about Jesus.

Inagori began going to the gaol to preach each Sunday morning, where there would be as many as 150 men in attendance. Many received Jesus and many sick men were healed as they learned that God could and would heal their bodies. As Inagori finished his year of high school and was ready to go home, the men at the gaol were saddened that he was leaving. They urged him to come to see them when he visited Goroka. They desired for their families to accept Jesus as their Savior also and receive the joy and peace they had.

While Inagori was in high school, he continued to study the Bible and improve his mastery of the English language. As he marked the words in his English Bible that were unfamiliar to him and looked up the meanings in the dictionary, he was aware of the presence of the Holy Spirit, our Helper. Since we often used him as an interpreter, he knew that he needed to understand English to accurately interpret our words into the local language.

In 1967 Inagori returned to Hageri where he taught in the school and continued to preach the Word to his people. They were excited to have one of their own boys leading them. And no matter what hour of the day or night, if they were sick they would ask him to come to their village and pray. Their faith in the God of the Word made them whole; He always honored His Word.

In 1968 Inagori and eight other young men began a year of

training in the English Bible school. He then went to Kainantu for a time to work with Brother and Sister Pearson.

How can you prove there is a God?

One day Inagori was walking through the jungle on his way to a remote village to minister when he met a man walking on the same trail. Inagori stopped to talk to him and told the man about God, but the man was very skeptical. He said, "How can you prove that there is a God that I might know that there really is a God?" Inagori responded, "I know that there is a God, and I believe that there is a God, and I will show you that there is a God." He continued, "Do you have any problem? Do you have anything that you cannot take care of? Is there anything that you would like God to do for you?"

The man thought for a moment. "Well, yes. I do have something," he said. "My wife was due to have a baby, but it's been several weeks and she still hasn't had the baby and she's not well at all. So, I do have that problem." Inagori responded, "I tell you what. We are going to pray right now. We are going to ask the Lord to deliver that baby the moment you walk back into your village. When you walk through the gate of your village and go up to the door of your house, your wife will start to deliver and have that baby."

They prayed. The man went on his way, and Inagori went on to the village. Later that week he saw the man again. The man said, "You know, you told the truth. Your God is real. The moment I got into the perimeter of my village and opened the door and entered my house, my wife started to deliver the baby. She had not been able to deliver this baby for a long time. So now I want to know more about this God that you told me about so that I might believe in Him too. I now believe that there is a God because you have proved that He does answer prayers."

So this man prayed with Inagori that he might receive Jesus Christ as his Savior. And he did. What a wonderful experience in the power of prayer!

THE ROMANCE OF INAGORI AND KAKINI

This story starts way back when we were living in Hageri and we had lots of converts that were going to the coastal town of Lae. There was no Foursquare church there. In fact there was no Pentecostal church in Lae at all. We wanted to go there to reach those people and to also reach the English-speaking young people of New Guinea. The government had built a technical college—a branch of the New Guinea University—in Lae. The students were all speaking English and there was not a Pentecostal church there to reach them. We applied for and got permission from the Mission Board to move from the Highlands to Lae and begin a work there.

Our policy has always been to have disciples training alongside us. We were not there to build a kingdom for ourselves but to establish churches and train leaders to take over those churches in order that the work may become totally indigenous. So we trained disciples to help in the ministry and to eventually take our place. One of these young men who was working with us in the Highlands was Inagori. He was very loyal and faithful and loved the Lord with all of his heart. He was very active in ministry and had several miracles occur within his ministry. He would witness to and pray for people, and signs and wonders would follow him. He was always witnessing to people and praying for people. So we asked him if he would be willing to come with us to Lae to start a new church and a new work.

He agreed to come with us, but he wanted to be married first. We thought that was a good idea because a wife would be able to help him a great deal. He told us that he had asked the Lord for a wife that could speak English. We raised our eyebrows on that request as we had never found any New Guinea girls who could speak English. He also told us that she would have to want to be a pastor's wife and she would need to be filled with the Holy Spirit. We knew that when anyone received Christ under our ministry, we led them to receive the baptism of the Holy Spirit as soon as possible.

In New Guinea marriages are traditionally arranged by the parents when the girl is very young. No consideration is given to the thoughts and feelings of the young people involved. As a result the tenderness of romantic love was unknown in their culture. A woman had to have a strong back to work in the garden, raise the pigs, and care for the children, and no thought was given to her comfort and convenience. When there were plenty of girls in the village, sometimes the parents waited until they were twelve or thirteen years of age before arranging for their marriage. But if there was a dearth of girls, then they dropped the age to nine or ten. The young people had nothing to say about the arrangements—it was a business agreement between the parents of the bride and the parents of the groom.

In the early days of the mission station the bride price was made up of pigs and shells; but after some natives had money or other valuables, these were included in the bride price. Some girls were worth more than others, but we never understood the reason for the difference. The bride price was paid by the father of the groom and displayed in the middle of the village. The young girl was brought to stand beside this display. It was at this point that the young man learned who would be his wife. When this engagement was announced, they usually had a big feast of *kaukau* and pig meat provided by the father of the bride. A father would not kill all the pigs he had for this wedding feast, because he must always keep some in reserve in case there should be a funeral for some member of the family. The natives had a high mortality rate, so death came often.

When the feast was concluded, the bride would tell her parents and her friends good-bye. Although she might be only a little girl of nine or ten, she had to leave her mother's hut and go to live with her future mother-in-law. The couple did not live together as man and wife until she came into womanhood. She raised pigs for her future husband and made a garden to supply him food. When she reached maturity, sometimes they had another small ceremony. A long piece of sugar cane was brought. The girl took a bite off of one end. The man bit off the other end. When their eating was finished, they were considered married.

Because of his close association with us, Inagori realized that we had exercised the privilege of choice in selecting each other. During the year Inagori spent in Australia, he observed that in other lands and other cultures young people were not compelled to permit their parents to choose their marriage partners. In any event, when Inagori saw a young lady that attracted him, he too desired to have the privilege of choice. He prayed and tried to find a way to free himself of the old traditions.

So it was that in the face of tribal customs, Inagori was in conflict. He found a girl to be his wife and he would have to break tradition. Kakini, the girl who had aroused Inagori's interest, lived in a village very close to Kapakamarigi, where the missionaries held their youth camps and conventions. Kakini attended church at Kapakamarigi and accepted Christ as Savior. She attended the Foursquare Youth Camp. It was at this time that Inagori and Kakini saw each other, but they did not talk to one another as they were both very shy.

At the beginning of the school year, Inagori was asked to teach at Hageri in the day school. During the weeks that followed, he thought much about Kakini. Finally he wrote her a letter and told her that he liked her and felt that she was the one for him. She was thrilled when she received the letter as she felt the same way about Inagori. She replied immediately telling him of her feelings toward him. From then on they corresponded frequently

Kakini was one of eight children. Her parents were Christians. After a few weeks Inagori went to Kakini's village to talk with her parents about marrying Kakini. According to New Guinea custom, this concerned not only Kakini's parents but also the men of the village who had helped to raise Kakini. They would receive some of the pay for Kakini. When Inagori asked the price they wanted for Kakini, they said $800.00. They told Inagori they did not want him to marry Kakini because he could not pay the money. Five months passed and there was much talk back and forth.

One day Inagori went again to the village to talk to all the men. And again he expressed his desire to marry Kakini. The men refused. But something unexpected happened, for Kakini, who had been silent to this point, spoke up. "But I want to marry Inagori. It is God's will and we are meant for each other," she said with great conviction. It took a lot of courage for Kakini to speak out. According to New Guinea customs, women do not have anything to say about their marriage. For Kakini to express herself in such a fashion was unthinkable! Inagori and Kakini had prayed much about this and they knew that God would undertake for them. Finally, after much talking that day, the men agreed that Inagori could marry Kakini if he paid them $400.00. Inagori felt that he could pay this amount. The young people thanked God for answering their prayers. Kakini took one year's training at Hageri in the English Bible school, and graduated just before they were married.

We had moved on to Lae before Kakini came into Inagori's life. Before long we got word that Inagori had found the girl he had prayed for. She was a member of our church in the Kapakamarigi area, she had learned English, she was baptized in the Holy Spirit, and she desired to be a pastor's wife—all the things Inagori had prayed for. Inagori asked us to come back to Goroka to the Highlands to perform the marriage ceremony. So we did, and Mason officiated. After a brief stay at their village, they moved to Lae to work with us and eventually pastor the church there.

Susanne Miracle

This is the story of Susanne Miracle. When Inagori and Kakini got to Lae, they stayed in a little temporary house that we had built just for them close to us as they adjusted to a new style of living, a new culture, the culture of the city of Lae. The people speak a different language, as well as Pidgin. The diet in Lae was different because it was on the coast and would consist of fish, rice, and coconut as opposed to the Highlands diet of sweet potato, vegetables, and some pig. Everything was going to be different for them. They told us later they had agreed that until they were able to get settled into the culture, they would prefer not to have a baby. So they asked the Lord to watch over that and not allow them to become pregnant until they had effectively integrated into the new coastal culture. Everything went well with that.

We got a permanent house built for them, and they settled

in fine. The work was steadily progressing and they were happy with how things were going, so they decided to ask the Lord for a child. Soon they became pregnant. About a week before the child was due to be born, Inagori came knocking on our door one Sunday afternoon and asked us to come and pray for Kakini. As we entered their house, we found her lying on the floor unconscious. We thought we would just lay our hands on her and pray and she would get up and be alright. We did lay our hands on her and all of us prayed, but she did not regain consciousness.

Lae was the second largest city in New Guinea, so it had a hospital, a telephone system, and other basic public services. We decided we should get Kakini to the hospital as quickly as possible, so we called the emergency ambulance and they came and took her to the hospital. We went along with them. The doctors examined her very thoroughly and told Inagori that it wasn't a good situation. The baby was dead in the mother's womb. The toxic poison from the dead baby was what had caused Kakini to become unconscious. They didn't know if Kakini would ever regain consciousness. They could not remove the dead baby at that time as there was no surgeon there. They would have to fly in a surgeon the next day at first daylight. He would be able to remove the dead baby and try to revive Kakini.

There was nothing more we could do, so we went home. Inagori said that he would have a talk with the heavenly Father. He prayed, "Father, I asked for a wife and a baby, and You have given me those. And now the doctor thinks they may be taken away from me. Lord, I know they are both Yours. But there is another problem You have, Father. There are nine men that have come from my village in the Highlands to the coast to celebrate the birth of my baby. They are watching. I have told them about the miracles that You do. So, Father, You have nine men that are watching You; and You have to take care of that." Mason thought, "That is pretty good. Give the problem to God. Let's not take it on ourselves." The Word tells us to cast "all your care upon Him, for He cares for you" (1 Pet. 5:7). So Inagori had this talk with God and went off to sleep.

The next morning we had to go to the Highlands to speak at the annual convention, so we were hurrying to load up and go. Inagori went to the hospital early in the morning. When he arrived the doctors explained that the surgeon had come and had removed the dead child, a little girl, by Cesarean section. They had put her in a box, which they had placed up on a shelf. The doctors presented Inagori with the death certificate for him to sign. Inagori said, "Well, I must see the baby before I sign this certificate." The doctors warned him, "You do not want to see the baby. It would be most unpleasant for you. The baby has been dead all this time, and we did not bother to wash the corpse. It is a dead child lying in a box."

"No, I must see it," Inagori insisted. So at his persistence, the doctor bought the box down off the shelf and set it on the table for Inagori to see the baby. He walked over and looked in the box. The moment he looked into that box, two hands immediately extended outward toward him and the baby began to cry. He looked at the doctor and smiled. He said, "Look, she is praising the Lord!" The doctor was astounded. He asked, "Who are you?" That doctor thought Inagori was the greatest witch doctor he had ever seen! Inagori said, "No, sir. I am a Christian, and my God does things like this." The doctor said, "Well, sir, your God has not done very much, because this little girl will be nothing but a vegetable all her life. So what you have done is not a great thing at all."

Nevertheless, they cleaned up the baby and washed her off. They took her into Kakini, who had now regained consciousness, and she began to nurse the child. Inagori and Kakini decided that they would name that child Susanne Miracle. Well, Susanne Miracle grew up and went to school. She was an honor student every year. She graduated elementary, middle, and high school with honors. She graduated from technical college and became the secretary for the minister of education over the entire country of Papua New Guinea. She became a living testament of how our God does miracles. She is now married and has children of her own and a wonderful ministry of serving the Lord in the local church and the marketplace.

As for the nine men, they witnessed this entire event. Those nine men went back to their villages and began to testify of the power of God to everyone that they came across. They testified to God's power to not only raise the dead but to give life to a dead baby who was taken out of the womb and sitting in a cardboard box on a shelf! And through these nine men, several churches were started in the Highlands.

As we reflect on that story, we admit that we were disappointed when we prayed and our prayers were not answered immediately. But God always answers prayer. He answers it the best way, and only He knows what is best! The better way for Him to answer that prayer was for Him to perform that miracle in order that many people would come to know Him. In fact, people in that hospital who were sick heard of this and they asked for Inagori to come pray for them. One man had collapsed lungs due to an extreme case of tuberculosis. Inagori prayed for him and both his lungs were restored back to full health again. Several others were healed. A hospital ministry was born from this miracle. Our church was invited to come every first Monday of the month to pray for the sick in that hospital. A group of people from our church would go to that hospital to pray for all those that desired healing.

A LISTENING HEART

A flat tire

This miracle has to do with a flat tire. Inagori was driving the Foursquare church's bus down the road out of Lae. The dirt and gravel roads are very bad in New Guinea—full of rocks, potholes, and all kinds of debris. The youth and teens would add to the problem by throwing empty soft drink bottles on the road and breaking them. Roads were not maintained and never policed for foreign items. Flat tires were a common occurrence. As Inagori traveled down the dirt road, he noticed he had a slow leak and was about to have a flat tire. He slowed down and prepared to pull over into the next filling station. But the Lord spoke to Inagori and said, "Not this filling station. Do not pull in here." So he went on. When he came to the next filling station, he thought, "Well, I better pull in here because my tire is running out of air." But the Lord spoke to Inagori again, "No, not this station." So he went on to the next station. The Lord said, "Okay, this one." So he pulled into the gas station.

When he came to a stop, the attendant noticed the Foursquare church's logo on the side of the twelve-passenger bus. He said "Are you a pastor?" Inagori answered, "Yes, I am." The attendant said, "I have been sitting here all morning thinking what it would be like to be a Christian. I would like to be a Christian, but I don't know how to become a Christian. I've heard people talk about being a Christian and what it was like to be a Christian, and I decided this morning that I would really like to know what it's like to be a Christian. But I have no one to tell me. Would you tell me?" Inagori said, "I sure will."

So, Inagori told him he was there to have the tire repaired. The attendant gave the tire to one of the workers to start the repair. While the workers repaired the tire, Inagori witnessed to the attendant. Inagori explained the blessings of becoming a Christian. He explained how to become a Christian by believing in the Lord Jesus Christ and inviting Him to come into your heart. So he prayed with this young man that he might receive Jesus Christ as his Savior. And he did.

This is a wonderful lesson in obedience. Sometimes we don't listen to the Lord; we do our own thing. But we need to learn to listen to the voice of the Lord and then obey. He will lead and guide us at all times—even when we have a flat tire.

The policeman by the side of the road

Inagori would frequently take the church's twelve-passenger bus to haul people to and from the church. He most frequently used it to pick up students from the university in Lae as students had no transportation. A lot of the young people wanted to come to the Lae church because of the contemporary worship style and the message in English. So Inagori would go out and pick up students and others who would come.

Lae Foursquare Church, built by Mason

Coming back to church one evening, Inagori spotted a policemen sitting on the side of the road. The policeman was not doing anything. Inagori was prompted to stop and ask, "Would you like to go to church with us?" The policeman said, "Yes, I would like to go." So the policeman got into the bus and came to church with Pastor Inagori. He heard praise and worship that he had never heard before. He noticed that everybody was so happy and clapping their hands and singing.

Then he heard Inagori speak about Jesus. He had not heard the message about Jesus like that before. He heard that Jesus loves you, that Jesus can help you. He heard that Jesus can make you have a better life. He heard that Jesus can even heal you when you are sick. So that policeman came forward after Inagori finished preaching and asked that he might receive this Jesus also, that he might have everlasting life, and that he might have a home with Jesus in heaven forever. And he asked for all the things that he could remember that Pastor Inagori preached about. So Inagori was able to lead this policeman to the Lord. The policeman was so happy that Inagori had listened to the prompting of the Lord and stopped to pick him up and bring him to church. And from that time on, that policeman was waiting on the side of the road on his days off so that Inagori could pick him up and take him to church so that he could learn more about the Lord Jesus Christ.

Eight cents to nine dollars

Inagori was blessed with a full life of ministry. He was an outstanding minister and diligently performed his pastoral duties. He was a great man of faith and the Lord blessed him with many miracles. This time Inagori experienced a miracle concerning his obedience to the voice of the Lord and His provision of food.

Inagori consistently called upon the people of Lae and often prayed for them. He was faithful to do this on a daily basis. When he got home this time, around lunch time, he began to prepare his lunch only to discover there was no food in the cupboard. It was dry and bare. So he sat down in the house and prayed. He asked the Lord to send him some food. While he was sitting there, which he had done many times before, he recounted the many times that the Lord had answered his prayer and would prompt someone to come by and bring them food to eat.

Sitting at his table, the Lord spoke to his heart and said, "Inagori, what are you doing sitting there?" "I'm sitting here because we have no food and the children are coming home from school and I must have some food to give to them. I'm waiting for someone to bring me some food or maybe give me some money so I can go buy some food." So the Lord said to Pastor Inagori, "When do you need that money?" And he thought for just a moment and he said, "I don't need the money sitting here. I need the money when I buy the groceries and have to pay for them."

So he said to Kakini, "Get your purse and let's go to the store and buy some food." She responded, "You know I only have eight cents my little string bag and there is no need in going because that will not buy anything." "Yes," Inagori told her, "bring your little string bag with your eight cents and let's go to the store." So they went down to the store. They walked up and down the aisles, and they bought all the things that they would need to have a lunch and prepare dinner for the children.

When they came up to the lady in charge, they proceeded to check out. So the cashier put the price in and cranked the handle for each item (they had no cash registers to check out and total a bill, all the stores had were manual hand-cranked adding machines). Finally, when totaled, all their groceries came to exactly nine dollars. So Inagori said to his wife Kakini, "All right, open your purse and pay for the food." She responded, "You know there is only eight cents in my little string bag." "No, the Lord said I only needed the right amount of money when I bought the food. We just bought the food, so we need the money right now. The right amount will be in your little string bag." So she opened up her purse and took out her little string bag. As she opened it, money began to fall out on the counter. Exactly nine dollars fell out on that counter in front of the cashier.

In this case the money came when they were buying the food. But this lesson can extend to anything. In other words, if you have faith for something, your faith will be manifested to action. Faith works when you begin to act on your faith rather than just sitting around waiting for something to happen. If you want rain, pray for it and then carry an umbrella!

A man after God's own heart

It is a matter of great concern for missionaries to find a native who has not only a desire to be a faithful witness to his people but also is a man who has the dedication, the mental ability, and a teachable heart—one who will take the training necessary to assume independent leadership in the event a day comes when they are no longer there to direct. Inagori demonstrated these qualifications well. Inagori's appetite for learning was whetted by the encouragement and wise guidance of various missionaries, and he availed himself of every opportunity to pursue the true wisdom and knowledge that comes from God. Only eternity will reveal the scope of his influence as a teacher, a leader, and a true missionary to his people. God saw the desire of Inagori's heart, when as a small child he declared: "I want to be a missionary!" and in His providence He brought it to pass. Inagori had a listening heart; he was a man after God's own heart. All to the glory of God are many assorted and amazing testimonies that came as a result of the preaching, prayers, and obedience of Inagori. His heart is reflected in Psalm 40:8: "I delight to do Your will, O my God."

Inagori and Kakini had four girls born into their family: Susanne, Triphina, Sondra, and Sharon. He and Kakini faithfully served in the Lae Church until 1979.

Inagori, Kakini, Susanne Miracle, Triphina, and Sondra

Chapter 10
METIKAU'S CALL TO SERVE GOD

*Most assuredly, I say to you, he who believes
in Me, the works that I do he will do also; and
greater works than these he will do.*
—JOHN 14:12

ETIKAU CAME TO US as a young boy. The people of Papua New Guinea did not have a calendar or any dating system. They never tracked their own age or celebrated birthdays. We estimated him to be about seven years old when he came with Inagori to the mission station at a Hageri. Because he was from Gotomi, a long way away, we let him stay at the mission station.

After he went through elementary school and graduated from Bible school training, Metikau became a wonderful worker for the Lord. During the time of his Bible school training, he became old enough to marry. As was the custom of the day, the parents had arranged a wife for him to marry. But she was not a Christian woman, and he did not want to marry her. His parents kept on insisting that Metikau leave his Bible school training. They kept stressing to him, "You must leave this school. You must go home to the land that has been allotted to you. You must build a fence around it. You must build a kunai grass and bamboo home on it. And you must marry and settle down." But he knew in his heart that he didn't want to do that. He wanted to finish Bible school training.

But one day, because of the constant pressure from his parents, he thought in his heart, "All right I will finish this year in Bible school, and then I will go home. Maybe I can come back and finish Bible school later." That night he was awakened by the Lord and given a scripture. He got up, got his Bible, took his little lamp, turned it up, and found the scripture. It was John 4:35: "Don't you have a saying, 'It's still four months until harvest'? I tell you, open your eyes and look at the fields! They are ripe for harvest" (NIV). He realized the Lord was speaking to him about not making the decision for himself that he was going to put off finishing Bible school training and do the will of his parents. This time the will of his parents was not the will of God. So he decided that he would obey the Lord and that he would go on with his Bible training.

All of us have some similar type of tests in life. The Lord never tempts us, but He does test us quite often to check our sincerity and our faithfulness. So the Lord spoke to Metikau about that same time and said, "I want you to go up to the village up on the mountain there and I want you to tell them about Me because they have never heard and they don't know what it means to be saved." So Metikau told his father that he was going to go up on this mountain to these people. His father retorted, "Absolutely not! You cannot go there because we have been enemies with those people and they will kill you because they will recognize you!"

All the New Guineans had certain tattoo marks on their face—some were on the sides of their face, some on their forehead—and those marks identified the tribe that person belongs to. The father repeated, "They will recognize you and they will kill you." Metikau said, "No, they won't. God has asked me to go, and certainly God is with me and will protect me." So finally the father said, "Well, all right. If you insist that you must go, I'm going to send someone with you." Metikau said, "Well, that's okay, but he cannot carry a bow and arrow because he will have to come like I'm going—without weapons. We are going in peace." So finally his father consented to how Metikau wanted to go up to this enemy mountain village.

It was quite a long way, and Metikau had to negotiate the lowlands before he started his climb up the steep mountain. While doing so, he met a little girl leading a woman by the hand. Metikau stopped to talk to them and found out that this woman was blind and that she had never heard about Jesus. So he began to tell her about Jesus and witnessed to her about the Lord and she opened her heart to the Lord. And then he said, "Now let us pray for your eyes." He said, "If you can believe, the Lord will heal." So he prayed and then asked, "Can you see?" And she said, "No." So he prayed a second time and inquired, "Can you see now?" And she said, "No, I can't." "Well," he said, "I'll do this one more time. After all, this is not what I'm sent to do. But if you will believe, God will heal you." So he prayed again. And she said, "Well, I'm sorry. I see tiny little bits but I can't make out anything." "Well," he said, "I have to go because I am on a mission, but you believe and God will heal you."

So he finished his talk with her and started again on the trail. As he was going up the mountainside, his curiosity began to arise, and his thoughts centered on his own actions. He began to think about what *he* was going to do when he arrived at the village. He realized that he was arriving at the perfect time. The young men would be out on hunting fields, the older men would be babysitting the small children, and the women would all be out in the gardens tending to the sweet potato. "I'll be able to make peace with the older men before the young men come back. This will be an excellent time for me to arrive," he reasoned. So momentarily he has forgotten that he is on a mission for the Lord and ponders on what *he* is going to do instead of what *God* is going to do.

It came as a shock when he finally arrived at the village and climbed up over the ladder gate to go into the village. Most villages have a bamboo type fence around the village to keep the wild pigs and other wild animals and unwelcomed people out. When he climbed over the top of the fence, to his amazement everyone was in the village. The women were there, the young men were there, and the old men were there. The moment he climbed up on that ladder and looked into the village, the young men saw him, drew their bows and arrows, and came running towards him to kill him.

The chief was there also. The chief told the young men, "Wait just a moment. Let us see what he has to say." So the young warriors retracted the arrows in their bows. Metikau said, "I have come to tell you a story about a Man who loves you—a Man who is called Jesus; a Man who can help you; a Man who is a good spirit and not a bad spirit like the witch doctors." The chief commented, "When I got up this morning, I felt impressed to make everyone stay in the village today. I did not know why." Then he instructed the young men, "Put your arrows away and let us hear what more he has to share." So Metikau went into the middle of the village where they gathered all the people together and they came around and found places to sit. The women always carried their small children and their babies in a string bag that they made called a *bilum*. The mothers would hang their *bilums*, with their baby inside, on little twigs and small tree branches while they sat down to listen to the words. One lady hung her *bilum* with her little baby in it on a small branch on the side of a tree, and she sat down to hear the message.

So Metikau gave them the beautiful story of how Jesus loves them. He explained how Jesus died for them and how Jesus shed His blood that they might have forgiveness of sin so that they might experience His love and that they might have a better life and have peace among themselves. All they had to do was believe and receive Him. When he was about to finish, he asked if anybody wanted to receive Jesus as their Savior. Unexpectedly, the small branch that had the little baby hanging on it broke, and the baby fell onto a rock at the base of the tree. He fell and struck his head against the rock. The mother picked up her life-less baby and began to scream and cry.

The young men grabbed their bows and arrows again and came running and said, "You see, he is an enemy, and we have let him come into our midst. The spirits are angry and they have killed one of our children and they will kill all of us if we don't get rid of him." As this was happening Metikau had taken the little baby from the mother, cuddled him in his arms, and prayed and asked God to restore life and wholeness back to this little child. And in front of all of them while they were looking on, they saw the swelling on the baby's head go down and life come back into this little boy. The little boy returned to normal again. Metikau handed the baby back to his mother. The chief said to the young men again, "Put your arrows away." So, for the second time, they put their arrows back in their sheaves and did not kill Metikau. Metikau went on with the message of Jesus and prayed for them. Several came to know the Lord that day. He stayed another day and many more came to know the Lord as their Savior. So the gospel was brought to this village through Metikau and his obedience.

But God was not finished yet. On his way home, Metikau experienced such a joyous feeling that he was able to bring the story of Jesus to these villagers who had never heard before. As he got to the bottom of the mountain and once again traveled through the lowlands, he saw a lady walking around. This lady called out to him and asked, "Are you the young man that went through here a couple of days ago?" He responded, "Yes." She said, "I am the lady you prayed for. It wasn't long after you left that the Lord opened my eyes. Now I can see, and I've been waiting for you because I wanted to thank you for what you did."

So that is the beginning of Metikau. He was able to marry a wonderful young Christian girl and they have a beautiful life together. There were many other things that the Lord allowed him to do. Metikau finally graduated and we appointed him to a church in Kapakamarigi.

Metikau and wife and children; a faithful pastor

METIKAU PRAYS, 500 FED

Because of the large numbers of young people being attracted to our ministry, we decided to develop a venue to cater to their specific needs. We designed a youth camp for these young people. Quite a few young people attended these youth camps. The campground had plenty of real estate. There were areas where the young people could compete in sports and play games. We had a large building that we met in and a church building. As the youth came, they would cut the kunai grass and construct temporary little huts to live in during that week of camp. These huts were all over the place, and we didn't mind them doing this at all. All our missionaries would attend the camp and help train and teach the youth by sharing Bible stories. Many, many young people came to know the Lord during the youth camps.

We fed those that participated because they didn't have any money to buy food. On one occasion during the last day of the camp, the cook came to young Pastor Metikau. The cook was rather concerned and told Pastor Metikau that he should go and get Mr. Hughes. The cook explained that they didn't have but a half cup of rice and they had 500 children to feed before they went home. He explained to Pastor Metikau that Mr. Hughes must drive into town and purchase additional rice. The cook didn't realize that town was quite a long way. Pastor Metikau replied, "Well, Mr. Hughes is teaching and we don't have time to wait until after he finishes. So, let's just pray." Metikau remembered how the Lord had multiplied food on different occasions and how even in the Old Testament the prophets had multiplied food. So he encouraged the cook to fill up the big cauldron with the normal amount of water and to put in the half cup of rice. The cook did so. They prayed that God would multiply that rice and make it enough to feed all the young people so they could eat before they went home.

Pastor Metikau dismissed the cook and went back to teaching his class. The cooks went about their business of preparing the dining room. Sometime later curiosity began to rise up within their hearts, so they went over and peered into the cauldron. As they lifted the lid off, they discovered that the cauldron was full of rice and pushing up the lid. That cauldron was so full of rice that it was actually pushing the lid up and almost off. God once again performed a great miracle.

Rock Band, Beer, and Fire from Heaven

It wasn't long after Metikau began pastoring the church in Kapakamarigi that things started to change drastically in Papua New Guinea. The previous government had not allowed any kind of alcoholic drink to be served to the New Guineans because of their inability to understand what it was and how it would affect their body and their mind. But that changed. A recently elected new government allowed the New Guineans to have alcoholic drinks and beer. Certain government officials decided to take advantage of the large space next to the youth camp at Kapakamarigi and arranged to bring in a rock band to perform a rock concert. In preparation for the concert, they came and built a compound of several small grass huts and some big houses with thatched roofs that would be shelter from the sun for the large groups of people. They were intending to bring their rock band and entice the young people to party by offering them free samples of beer. The beer company wanted to use this location and a rock band venue to encourage the local people to buy their alcoholic beverages.

When Pastor Metikau heard all about this, he got his people

together, his churches together, and his young leaders together and told them not to go near the concert. He told them to not have anything to do with it. He stressed for them to not go inside that compound. He explained, "The government officials have established a group of people to come inside and distribute free alcohol. Don't go in there because what they're doing is bad and is not good for you." So they prayed. And he said, "We are going to be praying the whole time they are here. And we're going to pray and ask God to do something to discourage them and to keep the young people away so that they will not be able to bring beer and establish a store here to sell strong alcohol to the people of this area." So they prayed more. And they were all praying together.

But we know how young people are. Some of them decided they would go down just to see what was happening. They didn't go inside but they sat on the edge of the compound looking at what was happening. And it wasn't long until they began to see something out of the ordinary happening. They were horrified and astounded to see fire coming down from heaven. The flames stopped about two feet above the grass roof. The flames were leaping up and down close to the grass roof over these people's heads.

When the participants of the concert came out and saw what was happening, they got frightened and begin to scream and yell, "What's happening? What's happening?" The young people told them, "Our pastor is praying to God that God would do something to discourage you people so you would leave." So the participants grabbed their things; they grabbed their battery-powered rock band guitars, their microphones, their stage props, and up and off they went.

And God saved that area from being invaded with strong

alcohol. Through much fervent prayer, God fulfilled Metikau's request. God did not want these people to be distracted at this time because God wanted the best for the people. God wanted the people to have life everlasting and wholeness and health and to use the little money that they had to use for wholesome things like food and clothing. They didn't need to throw it away for strong alcohol that would make them do silly things. And this is just another story of many about Pastor Metikau's work in that area.

Chapter 11
MIRACLES, GOD'S TESTIMONY

Heal the sick, cleanse the lepers, raise the dead, cast out demons. Freely you have received, freely give.
—MATTHEW 10:8

I T IS IMPORTANT to realize that the miracles that Jesus performed that are recorded throughout the Word and the miracles in our lifetime always have far-reaching results. The miracle has far more ramifications than just the fact that someone is healed or even raised to life. Miracles are a testimony of the power of God and the love of God. Miracles always bring forth greater works and advancements for the kingdom of God.

In 1966 miracles began to happen quite frequently. Many wonderful experiences took place because of the baptism of the Holy Spirit upon the pastors and ministry leaders of New Guinea. Miracles were commonplace. Blind eyes were opened, the deaf began to hear, and people were instantly healed from pneumonia and malaria, quite a common ailment in the Highlands of New Guinea. A young man with leprosy was healed. The crippled were healed. Natives with dysentery were healed. Even the dead were often raised alive again.

HEAL THE SICK, CLEANSE THE LEPERS

Deaf boy healed

In September of 1959 we had a chief and his wife to come and receive the Lord. When that happens, the people of his village always want to follow. The chief is their leader, and he often sets the example for his tribe of people. When the entire village receives the Lord, a church is built. We have churches that were started in different villages solely due to the leadership of the chief. On this particular Sunday, there was a young man who came to receive Christ during the altar call. So Mason called Sam over to him to talk in his Agapo language. He told Sam to tell the boy that we would lead him in prayer and he was to repeat what we said. So we spoke, and the boy didn't say anything. He didn't repeat what Sam said. So we talked louder, and he still didn't repeat anything. So Mason told Sam to speak louder and he spoke louder. The boy still didn't respond to either one of us.

Finally one of the members of the tribe spoke up and told Sam that the boy could not hear. He was indeed deaf. He had never been able to hear. He was deaf from birth. Sam and Mason agreed, "He needs to be healed." We turned our attention then to praying for healing for this young man. This didn't have to be interpreted because Mason was praying directly to God. And he prayed for God to open this young man's ears so that he could hear. Then Mason turned back to Sam and said, "Now, Sam, you repeat after me." In an audible voice Mason prayed and Sam repeated after him in the Agapo language, and the young boy began to speak! For the first time in his life the boy was able to talk. He repeated the prayer of salvation. He asked the Lord to come into his heart and forgive him of his sin and to make him a new creature in Christ Jesus. What a wonderful miracle! What a wonderful miracle working God we have who does hear and answer our prayers!

We had a number of deaf people receive their hearing, a number of blind eyes opened, and many other wonderful miracles that God has done through the people of Papua New Guinea.

The people of New Guinea believed that if God ever did it for anybody, he would do it for them. And they began to call out to God to do those same miracles that they heard about from the Bible. Incidentally, it was about that time, in the 1960s, when miracles began to happen because the people themselves began to believe God and pray to God directly for all their needs.

Blind eyes healed

One day Mason was ministering in Kapakamarigi and a young boy whose eyes were clouded came and stood before him. He could not see anything. Cloudiness covered his eyes. Mason felt a spirit of compassion for him. So he quickly took him aside, laid his hands upon his head, and prayed in Jesus' name that He might remove the clouds from this young boy's eyes. He prayed that these eyes would become clear that he might be able to see. Immediately we saw these clouds disappear from his eyes, and his eyes became instantly clear. He went away with perfect sight. Praise the Lord for this wonderful thing that He did!

Leper cleansed

Often our baptisms were very large. On one occasion we had 500 people baptized. One day Brother Pearson was baptizing recent converts and a leper came and requested to be baptized. Brother Pearson prayed as he put him under the water, "Lord, let this man be another Naaman." (See 2 Kings 5:1–19.) When this leprous man came up out of the water, he was white as snow. His leprosy was healed! This was a healing that could not be denied or explained. There was no doubt about it. Many believed because they saw this thing happen. Miracles such as those recorded in the Bible are commonplace in New Guinea, for in this land where death is a frequent visitor, more than one funeral service has been halted because the dead have been raised to life. As a result, whole villages have accepted the gospel and have become Christians.

RAISE THE DEAD

A Christian lady in a non-Christian village

There was a lady who heard about a lively church that was in another village far away from where she lived. The custom of the day was that the ladies all met in the gardens and tended to the sweet potato. The women would talk about a lot of things as they tended the garden. One of the women was sharing about this rather lively church and how they worshiped a Man called Jesus. So this lady decided to go check it out and see what was going on. The next Sunday she walked to this other village, which was far from where she lived. She attended the morning church service and listened closely to the pastors talking about Jesus.

During the message she decided that she needed Jesus in her heart. She received the message, walked forward, and talked to the pastor. The pastor prayed for her, and she gave her heart to the Lord. Her countenance changed immediately. In the days that followed, she became a fervent Christian. She let her light shine brightly. She had a peace about her. She was always joyful. Though most of the people in her village were not Christian, she lived a life that was so outstanding that they knew that she was somehow different. The Bible says to "let your light so shine before men, that they may see your good works and glorify your Father in heaven" (Matt. 5:16). And this lady did exactly that. Her life was so different. Her speech was so different. Everything she did was so different. She stood out in her village.

Unfortunately, she became very ill and she died. By this time the government had instituted a ruling requiring villagers to bury their dead in the ground. The many traditions and customs they used to practice were replaced by governmental law. They used to eat their dead. They used to place their dead up in mountain caves. They used to put their dead on the sides of hills. They used to put their dead on top of a mountain and build a fence around the gravesite to prevent evil spirits from stealing the soul of the dead. They used to practice many primitive tribal rites. The government was trying to standardize burial practices by enforcing one procedure for registering and burying the dead. This new law required a casket be buried at least six feet under the ground.

So the men of the village dug a hole for the grave. They gathered timber to make some type of a box that they could place her body into. Each village always had some type of burial ceremony to honor the dead. And the head chief asked the people, "What type of ceremony do we have for this woman? This woman was not like us. She was different. We don't know what kind of ceremony to have for her. We need to honor the dead and bury her properly." So someone suggested he go down to the village where she attended the church and talk to them about this issue. "The pastor will tell us," the chief said. So he went down to the village and found the pastor and told him about this lady who had been attending his church. The chief explained that she was dead and they needed to bury her but they didn't know what type of ceremony to have. So the pastor said, "I will come and I will take care of that." The chief went back up to his village—the non-Christian village.

The next day, the pastor arrived at the non-Christian village and gathered everybody around the burial site. The pastor began speaking to the people about this woman's life—about her receiving Jesus and why she was so different. He explained that the difference was because of Jesus living in her life. He explained that she was a Christian and Christians are supposed to live that kind of life. And in the midst of speaking to the people, the pastor felt impressed in his heart by the Lord. The Lord said, "Just pray a prayer over this woman." The pastor paused and thought, "Well, I don't normally do that. And it's hard because we know that she is with Jesus." But the impression kept getting stronger and stronger. So finally the pastor just turned to her body and prayed, "Lord Jesus, You certainly have shined brightly through this lady's life. She demonstrated the love of God every day. And You also showed how You are a forgiver. You forgive men of their sins. You also promised that one day, if we really are Christians and we love You and serve You, You are going to come back and receive us to Yourself and we are going to be where You are forever. Now help these people to know that You are real. Amen."

And at that point in time, this Christian lady arose out of the box that they had made. God decided to put life back into her again. It was rather a surprise to all. No one was expecting this to be the way that God would prove to these people that He was real. But He did. The young men of the village all stood up and ran away very quickly. Everybody thought it was because they were frightened. But it wasn't but an hour or so later that they came back carrying sapling poles, kunai grass, and large bamboo poles they used to build houses. As they came to the place where they had dug the hole for the grave and were beginning to fill again with dirt, they said, "We want a building here like you have down there at your village." In other words, they had gathered building materials and wanted a church right there where that woman was going to be buried.

So they built a church over that grave. They requested a pastor to be assigned in that village. They eagerly wanted to know this Jesus who has power to raise someone from the dead. So the miracle of this Christian lady living in a non-Christian village was that God raised her back to life to prove to these people that she was truly a born-again person who belonged to Him and that His power is so great that He has control over all things.

Abazento dead for three days

This is a story about a lady who was dead three days. Her name was Abazento. She was from the village of Neumozafobe. This happened around 1965 or 1966. We had established a new Bible school at Kapakamarigi, and we had a day school operating at Hageri. We did the teaching early on but could not continue due to the abundance of other things demanding our attention. So, we prayed and asked the Lord to send us helpers. We soon had a lot of helpers. They came from Australia and many different places to New Guinea. We soon had a lot of teachers on the mission station. On Sundays, when there was no school, Mason would take some of the teachers with him and deposit them along the road at nearby villages while he went on to the furthest village to minister there. On the return trip he would pick them up and bring them back to Hageri.

On one particular Sunday when Mason came to Neumozafobe, he parked near the village. This place was behind Henganofi. When he walked back into where the church was, we all sat down. They had logs in the church that they would sit on. There was a little bench-like seat in the front where they would have Mason sit. He sat down on the bench, and they all began to gather. When the church was full, we started. Sometimes this took hours. The New Guineans don't have a clock or a timepiece like a watch. They don't know anything about time. They didn't know how to keep time. They go by the sun. When the sun is up, it usually is bright and early. When it is overcast and the sun is not showing itself, they are not too aware of what time it is. They would come strolling in at different times according to our time; but according to them, they were right on time.

Mason asked if anybody had any testimonies over the week. One lady stood up and stated, "I have a testimony." Mason asked her to share. She said, "I died and I was dead for three days and God brought me back to life." Mason encouraged her, "Tell me about that. Tell me what happened. Tell me the story." The young pastor who had been there was Pastor John. Mason soon came to find out that Pastor John had witnessed what happened.

This lady, Abazento, died while her husband was in the deep jungle hunting. The chief sent a couple of men to go find him and bring him back to the village so they could properly notify him of his wife's death and conduct a proper burial ceremony for her. The villagers had a little hut off to the side of the village where they stored her dead body. They laid her down in that hut and covered her with a blanket.

Pastor John went down to see how things were going. The other village women had come down with their bamboo knives that they used to cut and peel the sweet potato. They had come down to mourn and had already tied the rope vine around the joint of their finger. They were prepared to cut off a joint of their finger for Abazento, as this was the pagan tradition in New Guinea. If someone died in their family, the women would cut off a joint of their finger. They would drip the blood over the dead body to show the spirits that they were sorry for this death. That way the spirits would not come back to haunt the living. When Pastor John saw these ladies, he became very upset. He quickly stopped them and ran them out of the village. He told them to not ever do anything like that again. He explained to them that Abazento was a Christian woman and that they were Christians as well. He explained to them not to do such pagan practices anymore because that practice does not line up with the Word of God. God says you're not to cut and harm yourself like that (Lev. 19:28). So Pastor John ran them away.

He decided he had better keep watch because they might try to come again and do themselves harm. So he stayed there, praying and praying and praying. His prayer was mostly for the people: "Lord, do something to help these people to know that they are Christians and that they no longer need to follow the old pagan customs, the old traditions, especially cutting a joint off their finger. Help them to know that covering themselves with mud and doing all of these things that they would do when someone dies are pagan practices."

Pastor John continued his prayerful watch until about the third day, when the husband was found and came back to the village. It was early in the morning, just as the husband was entering the village, when Pastor John heard an unusual noise. He looked around and there was Abazento, sitting up and talking! God had put life back into her; and now she was sitting up, totally well again!

Pastor John interpreted as Abazento told Mason her part of the story. She began, "Oh, I've been on a long journey. I've been to a very beautiful place. The houses are so different than our houses. There are lots of them. In fact, I walked on streets...." She hesitated, not knowing how to describe them. Then she looked around to try and find something that would help her explain what she saw. Her eyes rested on Mason's ring. "I walked on streets like that!" she said excitedly as she pointed at his shiny gold ring. It was his wedding ring. She had not seen gold before. New Guinea men do not have gold nor do they wear rings of any type. She had never been told a description of heaven. And yet this illiterate woman, who could not read or write and had never seen a Bible, was telling us a detailed description of what heaven looks like— how beautiful it is, of its streets of shining gold, and of a strange and wonderful home that was there which had been built just for her.

Then she told us that she was asked if she wanted to go in to stay there in heaven; for, she said, "When you go in you must stay." She went on with her story, "I looked at everything and it was so beautiful. I do not have the words to describe it all. I wanted to stay. But I told them I have a little boy. 'I will go back and look after my young son, and then I'll come back another time.'" Jesus then told her, "Tell My people I am coming soon. I am indeed preparing a home for them." She continued the description of her journey, "Then I went down a long tunnel and black things tried to grab me, but they could not reach me. I was not afraid." And so it was at that time that she came back to life again and heard the pastor praying.

Pastor John was able to witness this as it happened. He reunited her with her husband and her little boy. She continued to raise her son. That boy grew up and attended our day school and our Bible school and has become a pastor of a Foursquare church in Papua New Guinea. Abazento has gone on to be with the Lord and is now living in her eternal home, the most beautiful home.

Abazento, who was raised from the dead, with her son

God had graciously let her be an example to all the people in that area of Neumozafobe. All the villagers witnessed the glory of God and the goodness of God. They heard a firsthand account of a place called heaven and understood that Christians do have a home there. Jesus said, "I go to prepare a place for you. And if I go and prepare a place for you, I will come again, and receive you unto myself; that where I am, there ye may be also" (John 14:2–3, KJV). So this became a reality to the villagers of Neumozafobe because one of their own had seen heaven.

Abazento testified, "What the missionary tells you is true because it comes from the Word of God." Though they didn't have it in printing and they didn't have it in writing, they believed the Word of God when they heard it: "The entrance of Your words gives light; It gives understanding to the simple" (Ps. 119:130). It was a great blessing when the Pidgin Bible was produced. And it was an even greater blessing when the children who were in day school learned to read English and could read the English Bible also. Now they have both the written and spoken Word of God, which "is quick, and powerful, and sharper than any two-edged sword" (Heb. 4:12).

Thank God for the power to raise the dead! Jesus gave instructions in Matthew 10 when He sent His disciples out to minister to heal the sick, cleanse the lepers, cast out demons, and raise the dead (v. 8). "All things are possible to him who believes" (Mark 9:23). So this is a promise that Jesus gave to those who believe.

Whatever you ask in My name

This miracle happened with Abarito Inoki, a school teacher who taught in our day school for the children at Hageri. Abarito had gone to her village on a school holiday. Since she was a teacher and a Christian, she decided to get all the children of the village together to tell them a story about Jesus. As all the children gathered around, she began talking to them. She searched her heart for the right story. Jesus lay upon her heart the scripture found in John 14:13, which says, "And whatever you ask in My name, that I will do." As she thought about that, she entitled her story, "I Know a Man You Can Ask Anything in His Name and He Will Do It." That's a very exciting title!

The children were so excited; they never heard anything like that before. So she began to tell them about Jesus, the Man that you can ask anything in His name and He will do it. And she began to share with them all the different things that she could remember that Jesus had done that were impossible for man to do. The children were so excited and everything was going so well. But just as she was about to finish her story, a man walked up from the men's quarters, the big ceremonial house that all the men shared with the young men, and walked all the way down to the village to the huts were his wife lived. He came out with a bundle in his arm, and he walked straight up to Abarito. She said, "Well, what is this?" He said, "I have been listening to you. You said that you know a Man that you can ask anything in His name and He will do it. Well, I brought my little daughter for you to talk to this Man and ask Him if He will heal her and make her well."

So she thought, "This is a wonderful thing. Now I can pray for this little girl and the Lord will heal her and all of the children will see that what I've been telling them is true—that I know a Man you can ask anything in His name and He will do it." So she reached out to take the little girl. The man folded back the blanket and she noticed that the little girl was not normal. So she asked, "What's wrong with this little girl?" "Oh," her father said, "she died yesterday, and we were going to bury her today.

But you know a Man that you can ask anything in His name and He will do it. So I have brought her to you."

Abarito stood there, wondering what she should do. She thought, "I've never seen anything like this, never been involved in anything like this." As she pulled her hands back rather than take the child, the Lord spoke very gently into her heart, "What have you been telling the children all morning?" And she remembered she had been telling the children that she knew a Man that you can ask anything. She stopped right there and reached out and took that little body in her hands. It was cold and stiff and blue. She closed her eyes, as she couldn't bear to look, and begin to pray and ask Jesus if He would heal this little girl and put life back into her again so that all those children that were there and this man would see the power of Jesus Christ. And as she prayed, she said she thought she felt warmth coming into her hands from this little body. So she opened one eye and looked at the child; and she saw an eye of the little girl begin to twinkle. And then both eyes opened. And then this little body came back to life. God put life into this girl so that all those children and that man and that whole village could see the power of God and hear the testimony of how God had healed a little girl and put life back into one that had been dead for over a day.

The man quickly ran to his house and came back with some chickens. He wanted to pay her. She said, "No, no! I didn't do this. My Jesus, the Man that I talked about, He's the One that did this and He will do this for anyone—not just for me." And so the man thanked her very kindly. He ran to his hut to return his daughter to his wife; but this time she was whole and well and fully alive because of the power that is in the name of Jesus Christ.

Maria's mother dies

This is a story about Maria. She was a Bible student at Gotomi. She was studying to be a pastor and help in the church of the village that she was from, which was about a day's maybe a day and a half walk outside of Farmo, depending on the weather. She would have to walk a few more hours to take the road that leads to Gotomi. Word came to Maria that her mother had died and that she must come home. So she got permission to leave from the dean of the Bible school and started off to walk the few hours out to the main road. Once she got to the main road, there were passenger trucks that she could hire. These are trucks that have benches in the bed of the truck. Passengers would get on the back of the truck bed and sit on the bench. They called them PMVs—passenger motor vehicles. That's the transportation they have even today. So Maria walked out to the road (for the natives the walk would be about two hours; for the average person it would take four hours) and waited for the PMV to come. From there she had about a two-hour trip down to her village road on the other side of Farmo. She would then have to walk from the main road back into her village, which would be another few hours depending on how fast she walked.

When she got back into the village, they showed her where her mother was lying, in a special little hut where they had placed her. Mourners were there. They had learned the Asian custom of hiring people to mourn and wail when someone had died. They didn't yet understand that as a Christian they didn't have to mourn and wail because this is not the last time they would see their loved one. If they are all Christian, their loved one would be in heaven where they would see them again someday.

So, when Maria walked into the village and they showed her where her mother was lying, she said, "I must go in and pray for my mother." They said, "Oh, she's dead. Why are you going to pray for her?" Maria told them, "As I was walking down the trail, I was very concerned. My mother is very young, and I was asking the Lord why she would have to die so young. And the Lord told me that if I would believe, my mother would come back to life again. So I must go in and pray for her." So Maria went in and prayed for her mother.

She came out and went into the hut where all the family was preparing for the burial. They were cooking sweet potato. She was eating some sweet potato when everyone suddenly noticed that the mourning had changed to shouting and rejoicing. They went to the door of the little hut to see what was happening. The hut was empty. They looked around. To their amazement, they spotted Maria's mother walking around in the village. So, after almost two days of being dead, the Lord raised her mother back to life again. Maria wanted to have her mother back, and the Lord told her, "If you will just believe, I will bring her back to life again." So Maria was able to go back to the Bible school and share the testimony of the power of the Lord Jesus Christ in raising her mother back to life again.

CAST OUT DEMONS

Don't chase the devil

Since Baieso had come down to us from Gotomi, we decided to go and talk to the people. We discovered that they really wanted and needed a school. So we started a school to teach them Pidgin and train them in the Word of God. We had to have someone there to do that teaching. So, two young ladies that were working at the mission station, Helen and Pauline, decided that they would go be the teachers for that school. Even though inaccessible by vehicle, they took it upon themselves to walk six hours from the road and cross the river to get to Gotomi. We built a house for the new lady teachers. With the help of the people, a school was constructed so we could educate the people and teach the children about Jesus. We also started a Bible school there to teach and train pastors to take the Word into the many villages in that surrounding area.

Graduates from our Bible School in Gotomi with missionaries Pauline and Helen

Mason would go every week and teach in the Bible school. When the girls got settled, they were able to do most of the teaching and Mason only went every second week, when he would see how they were doing and help them teach the Word.

Once when he was scheduled to go to Gotomi to preach the Word, Mason was walking on the tiny trail, and one of the natives touched him on the shoulder and motioned him to quickly stop. So he stopped immediately. He looked where the native pointed down just in front of his feet. There was a coiled up death adder lying on the trail. The death adder is a deadly viper, a little snake that lies with its tail on the trail. If anything touches its tail, it springs backwards and strikes. If Mason had taken one more step, he would have stepped directly on its tail and it would have sprung back and bit him. And it is a well-known fact that a person has about three minutes to live if bit by a death adder. If you get bitten by the death adder you die quickly, especially without an antidote. They are very poisonous and feared by all the people in Papua New Guinea. So Mason praised the Lord that He had seen fit to have one of the brothers with him to be aware enough to stop him from stepping on that snake.

The Lord be glorified for sparing his life! Of course there was a reason for that. The enemy did not want Mason to go in there and teach, especially with what was about to happen that day. When he arrived into the village of Gotomi, the girls were very upset. They were in their house with the door closed and Gotomi was empty. So they quickly received him in and he asked, "What's the problem? What is going on? Where is everybody?" They said a young demon-possessed boy had just come down from the jungle. This happened frequently. Possessed people were frequently brought to the mission station. We would cast out these demons in the name of Jesus. One thing that we came to learn was that when we did that, the demons would go possess someone else. So we learned early on that when we prayed for a demon to leave a person, we would command that demon not to return to a person and demand it go back to its place. So we slowly began to clean up that area by praying and preventing the demons from just jumping from one person to another.

This young boy was possessed by a demon, and he had come to Gotomi and was threatening everybody in the village. He threatened all the children that were in the school and even the missionaries. Just as Mason was approaching the village, he ran out of the village into the jungle. They said, "Well, he has been here all morning tormenting everybody; but when someone yelled and said that you were coming, the boy took off and left." So Mason asked one of them, "Where is he?" They said he had gone to his village. So Mason asked, "Can you show me where it is?" They answered, "Sure." So up the mountain trail we went, further and deeper into the triple canopy jungle. We finally got to his village and we asked, "Where is this boy?" They knew his name. "Where is this boy?" "Oh," they answered, "When he heard that you were coming, he ran away further into the jungle and he's not here anymore."

Mason thought, "Well, I know the enemy is trying to keep him away from us, but we will outsmart the enemy." So he asked the people, "Do you know how to get into the jungle where he is going." "Yes," they said, "we know." We started off further, deeper into the bush of the mountains of New Guinea. And we had only gone about maybe four or five minutes when the Lord spoke to Mason's heart and asked, "Is this what you came to do?" Mason thought, "My, my, my. This is *not* what I came to do." He was talking to himself and the Lord. "I came to teach the young men and women in the Bible school, and here the enemy has got me out in the bush chasing a demon-possessed boy. I didn't come to do that." So he turned around and said to the fellows with him, "Let's go back. We've got work to do." So we went back to the village of Gotomi. We met with all the young men and women that were there to learn that day, and we taught the Bible.

We had something to eat late that afternoon. We always have a village service; so we walked out of Gotomi into a nearby village, and we had our service that night. Many people received Christ as their Savior. Returning home we were walking back up the trail and someone called out, "Mr. Hughes." He answered, "Yes." "Are you still wanting to see that boy that you wanted to see this morning that was possessed with demons?" "Oh yes," Mason responded. They said, "He is in that hut right in front of you." As Mason stopped and looked around, he noticed a small hut right beside him. He told them, "Tell him to come outside." So they called him by name, and Mason commanded him to come outside. We prayed for him and the Lord delivered him from the demon power right then and there.

So the Lord knew all about how to take care of these things but the devil was trying to sidetrack us. The enemy will often try to get us sidetracked into doing something good and worthwhile but it is not what the Lord would have us to do. So we need to make sure we are always doing what God wants us to do. Then we will always have His protection. We will always have His blessing. We will always have His victory when we do what the Lord wants us to do. So when Mason turned around and went back to the Bible school to teach the students, the job he had come to do, that is when we saw victory and then is when we saw the boy delivered from the demon power that had overtaken him. Praise the Lord!

Patrolman Robert, Warden Haniel, and the wild one

This is the story about Robert the policeman. This miracle happened in Kundiawa. Robert was a policeman in the Sifu District and his headquarters was in Kundiawa. They had a primitive jail at the headquarters. A policeman's job in Papua New Guinea is a very serious job, primarily because of two codes or customs that the New Guineans lived by for centuries and that rule their relationships even to this day. The first is the "payback." If you hurt them, then they will pay you back by hurting you or someone in your family. If you kill someone, then another from that tribe would kill you or a member of your family. The second custom is the "*wantok* system." The word *wantok* literally means "one talk" or someone who speaks my language. The wantok system is that if we speak the same language, you have to do favors for me, and you will never harm me or kill me. So, if a policeman arrested someone who spoke his own language and took that person to headquarters, then it would be quite possible that they would be angry and could come at him or his family members under the payback and/or *wantok* system. So the policemen in New Guinea have hard jobs.

Robert was true to his job. He was a convert who had come to know the Lord through our mission station. He got a job as a policeman and was now working in the Chimbu district. On one occasion he brought in a man that had broken the law. He went to the police headquarters where his job was to turn this man over to Haniel. Haniel was the name of the warden who looked after the jail. Robert knew Haniel quite well. So Robert brought the man to the warden and the warden gave him to the assistant for booking. While they were booking the man, Robert spoke with Haniel about the Lord. And Haniel gave his heart to the Lord right then during their conversation. Haniel asked Robert when he got ready to leave, "What will I do now?" Robert replied, "I will come and get you on Sundays and I'll take you to church and you can learn what to do at church." So Robert went on Sundays and got Haniel and brought him down to the Foursquare church in Kundiawa.

Haniel heard all about the good things of the Lord—how the Lord saves, how the Lord heals, how the Lord has a gift to give you called the baptism of the Holy Spirit that will help you live a better life and help you understand His Word better. Haniel asked that he might receive this baptism of the Holy Spirit. So they prayed for him and he did receive the baptism of the Holy Spirit. He was so happy. So he returned home. The next day, word came from higher up in the mountains to Haniel that his uncle was very ill and they didn't expect him to live. The message encouraged Haniel to go and see his uncle before he died.

So Haniel thought, "Well, I saw that they were praying for the sick in the church. And the missionary said if you just go and lay hands on the sick and pray that God would heal them." Having this revelation, Haniel became anxious to go and see his uncle. He trekked up the mountain trail and came to the village where his uncle lived. He went inside and said, "Cheer up, Uncle. I have good news for you. I have some good medicine." The uncle said, "Please hurry up and give it to me because I am a very sick man. I cannot eat and I have not been able to walk for days." "Oh," Haniel said, "I don't have that kind of medicine. I have Jesus. Jesus can make you well." "Oh, I don't know about Him. Who is He?"

There were three other men that had come in the hut by that time, and they were listening to what Haniel was saying to his uncle. Haniel said, "Jesus is the Son of God. God is the Creator of all things. Everything that you see has been created by God— all of the trees and all of the animals and all the people and even the rains are from God. He created everything that is good. He is a good God and He wants to save you. He wants to help you. He wants to give you a new life so that you might have a better life. He wants you to have a home in heaven where He lives. He wants you to come live with Him." Haniel did not know a lot about the Word of God; but he had been to church a few times. He knew what the pastor had spoken about, and he was trying to relay that to his uncle.

Haniel continued, "I'm going to lay my hands on you and pray." So he did. He laid his hands upon his uncle and prayed a simple prayer that he had heard the pastor at the Kundiawa

Foursquare Church pray. And the Lord heard his prayer and healed his uncle. He immediately sat up and said, "I'm hungry. I would like to have some sweet potato to eat." So the three men that were there, dumbfounded and surprised, looked at the fire that was almost out because the uncle had not eaten anything. They began to blow gently on the coals and embers to stoke up the fire so they could cook some sweet potato. Still in total silence and amazement, they put some wood on the fire. It began to build up so they put some sweet potato in the fire to cook.

While the potatoes were cooking, the men said to Haniel, "That's amazing that you know how to pray and talk to this Man and that He will answer prayer and He will heal people." We have a young girl; she is about twenty years old. She went out of this village, and she is living in the wild. She crawls around on her knees and never stands up. She lives in an area where there are many rocks and gravel. She has pulled some bushes, trees, and branches together, and she hides in there and she will not come out. We go to see her to bring her food. We have to just throw the sweet potato near her so she will come out, grab it, and crawl back into her shelter and eat. She's lived that way now for all these months—many moons. Can this Jesus you're talking about help her?" Haniel looked at them and said, "Sure He can. He can help anybody. He loves all people. He can help her. When my uncle finishes eating, we will say good-bye to him and we will go up to where she is if you will lead me to her place." The uncle said, "I'm going too." But they said, "You are sick." The uncle said, "No, I am well now. I am going to."

So the four of them walked back into this jungle area where this young girl was living in the wild. They asked Haniel, "How are you going to talk to her? She won't respond." He responded, "I believe she will. I believe that Jesus loves her enough that she'll respond to Jesus." So Haniel stopped in front of the makeshift shelter where she had been staying all this time. Then he commanded her, "In the name of the Lord, come down here. I want to talk to you." She came right out and walked straight down to where Haniel was. The uncle and the two men with him were very surprised. They said, "She has never responded to us before."

We have no idea what she might've looked like, living in this condition for so many months without taking care of herself at all; but that didn't matter to Haniel. He just knew that God loved her and God wanted to do something for her. So he looked at this girl, and he prayed, "Jesus, heal her and make her well again." And that's all the prayer that he prayed. Jesus responded immediately and touched that young girl. Prior to that prayer, she was just squatting and kneeling on the grass—even eating grass. After that simple prayer, she stood up like a human and she began to talk. This was the first time she had talked in almost two years. As she began to utter words, she told Haniel how grateful she was that whatever had possessed her and held her back was now gone and she was free and she could speak. They didn't understand what had happened, but Haniel found out later from the pastor that this girl was demon possessed. The demons possessed her and held her in captivity all this time. And the prayer that he prayed was a prayer that Jesus heard and answered. So they went back from that place a joyful family. They took the young girl back to her village. They presented her to her family. Her family was so happy.

This is the way churches were usually started—with some kind of a miracle that Jesus performs. It introduced Him to the people as the God of power, the God of love, the God of healing, and the God of understanding. The people were unaware of how some teach that you must pray a special prayer using the right words for an exorcism and that you have to know how to do it and follow the protocol to conduct a successful exorcism. They simply believed that they didn't have to tell God what to do; God always knows what to do. So you just have to pray a simple prayer, "God, heal this girl and make her well again." That was all that was needed to be prayed. And that's what God did.

So Haniel stayed the night and went back to his work in Kundiawa a very happy man. He had experienced the power of the name of Jesus Christ. Now his uncle had found Jesus Christ. Now a young girl had been restored back to wholeness and health again, all because of the love of God and the love of Jesus Christ and the fact that Robert the policeman was not ashamed to tell Haniel about Jesus and introduce him to the Lord Jesus Christ. Praise the Lord.

Chapter 12
SOVEREIGN ACTS OF GOD

He does according to His will in the army of heaven And
among the inhabitants of the earth. No one can restrain
His hand Or say to Him, "What have You done?"
—DANIEL 4:35

GOD IS NOT limited by time or space or man's percep-
tions or understanding. He does what He wants when He
wants and how He wants to accomplish His purposes. He
is sovereign in the universe and in the lives of men. As Jesus said
to His disciples who were faced with what seemed an impossible
concept, "With men this is impossible, but with God all things
are possible" (Matt. 19:26).

GOD SPEAKS TO THE NIJUFA CHIEF

This is a story about a sovereign act of God at Nijufa. Nijufa was
in the Bena Bena area—an area that Mason had not yet explored.
We were just beginning the work in 1956, and we had so much to
do that we had put off getting to the Bena Bena. But God decided
it was time to reach those people with the Word. So one morning
when the chief of this area woke up, the Lord spoke to him and
impressed upon him the words, "Go to the Foursquare mission."
He asked everybody in his village, and nobody had ever heard
of the Foursquare mission. No one knew where it was. The chief
became very upset. He was so upset that he forbade anyone from
leaving the village until he got an answer. So, until someone

found out what those words meant, no one went anywhere. The words continued to stir in his mind. He was frustrated that he did not know what they meant.

Towards the end of the afternoon, God inspired a young man from another village to go on a hunting trip at the top of the mountains near the Bena Bena. While he was on this hunting trip, he saw another man. Now remember, they were headhunters in those early years and they were ferocious warriors. They had clear and distinct enemies that did not allow encroachment on their territorial land. They would not just stop and talk to anybody they met on the trail unless they saw a tribal marking on their face that they recognized was from a friendly neighboring tribe. This young hunter was able to see the tribal markings of the approaching tribesman and recognized them as friendly. He exposed himself from hiding and they began to talk. The man explained that he had just come from the Foursquare mission in the Dunantina valley. So they exchanged pleasantries and the men went on their way. The younger man went on to Nijufa.

As he came into Nijufa, he asked, "Why is everybody here just milling around? What's going on?" And the chief said, "I have these words in my mind that I am supposed to go to the Foursquare mission, but I don't know where the Foursquare mission is. I have never heard of anything like that." And the young man told the chief, "Well, I know. I just met a man on a hunting trip, and he told me where it was. I know exactly where it is." The chief was very pleased, "We must go first thing." It was getting late, so they agreed they would launch out early the next day. The next morning they got up and prepared to go. The young man was going to lead the chief over the mountaintop down into the Dunantina Valley where the Foursquare mission was. They began their trek and arrived just a little before lunch.

They found somebody they could talk to, who brought them to Mason. They told him their story. "I'm so happy," the chief said. "I will tell you why," Mason responded, "God loves you and God wants you to hear the story of salvation. He wants you to hear about how He can help you to become a better person, how He can help you to live a better life. He wants you to hear that He has a place prepared for you to live forever with Him in heaven where He is. *That* God is the Creator of all things. Everything you see around you, God has created. He even made you." And Mason explained to him as much as he could and as much as he could understand, through the interpreter, about God and God's love and that God wanted him to receive Him into his heart so that he would have his sins forgiven and that he would become a new man in Christ Jesus.

And so the chief decided, "Okay, I will try that. Since these words have been in my mind to come over here, it must be the right thing to do. This must be what the big Man in heaven wants me to do." So he invited his other men with him—about five of them—and they all came and kneeled down on their knees before Mason. Through the interpreter he encouraged each of them to ask the Lord Jesus to come into their heart and forgive them of their sins and for the Lord to make them a new person in Christ Jesus. And they all received the Lord.

And it's amazing how that these primitive headhunters, by receiving the Lord Jesus into their heart, have the very same experience that we have. In other words, it's the exact same emotional, mental, and spiritual experience. They become a new person in Christ Jesus. One of the scriptures that the Lord laid on Mason's heart early in the ministry was Psalm 119:130: "The entrance of Your words gives light; It gives understanding to the simple." So by giving the Word of God to these people and by them receiving it into their hearts brings the light. And the light of the world is Jesus Christ (John 8:12). It also brings understanding. Understanding is the work of the Holy Spirit. The Holy Spirit makes known to us what is right and what is wrong. And He will even lead and guide us into all truth (John 16:13). So the Word is so powerful. It says in the Bible that "the word of God is living and powerful, and sharper than any two-edged sword" (Heb. 4:12).

So the Word changed their appearance—not their physical appearance but the way they acted, the way they talked, and the desires they had. The chief said, "Oh, all my people must hear this in my own village." Mason encouraged them, "You spend the day here and tomorrow morning we will rise early and I will drive to Nijufa. I know where Nijufa is. It is in the Bena Bena area. That way you won't have to walk back over the mountain for several hours." And that thought was a thrill for those men because they had never ridden in a vehicle before. To ride in a Jeep was going to be a real experience for them. Mason asked, "Well, how far is it?" and they all looked at each other and finally one of them said, "Long way *lik-lik*." When they say "long way *lik-lik*," that means they don't really know. It literally means "it's a long way—a little." It's an expression that they use because they don't really know how to count. They only have two numbers— *magoki* and *taragi*, one and two respectively. They can put those together with their fingers and go to five; but if it is more than five, they put both fists together and just simply say, "It is more than anybody can count." So they didn't really know how far it was, but they said that it was not too far.

Mason told them we would go early the next morning. So

we got ready and got in the truck. The five of them piled in the bed of the truck where there was room for them. Mason put the chief in the front with him and his interpreter. We started out on the road to the area of the Bena Bena towards the village of Nijufa. We were told that when we got close to the village, there would be a large river, the Bena Bena River, which separated the road from the rest of the village. We would have to leave the truck there and go on foot to cross the river to get into the village. We drove on and on—past noon, and we still weren't there. Finally, eight hours later in the late afternoon we arrived at the river.

So we left the truck and forded the river. They wanted to carry Mason across the river. Two men stood side by side, and he sat on their shoulders. When they would drift apart a little to where he was almost falling, he would get ahold of their hair and pull them back together again until we reached the other side of the river. We soon walked into the village. When they heard us coming, all the women looked up. They saw a white man, and they did not know what to think. They didn't know what had happened or where he had came from. So they grabbed all their children and began to run into their huts and hide. They had never seen a white man before. They thought he was a spirit. After all the excitement and commotion, some explaining, and a lot of them touching Mason's skin and hair, we all got settled in.

We got everybody out of the huts and gathered them together to have a meeting with all of the people in this village. And quite a number of them, when they heard the story of Jesus, received Jesus into their hearts. Not everyone received, but quite a large number of them did receive Christ into their hearts. Then the chief said to Mason, "Now you must come back more often. You must help us to understand and know this God that we have received into our hearts and into our lives." So he began to go back and minister to them on a weekly basis.

We established a training program at Hageri where we were training pastors, so we assigned a pastor to that area. The people of that village decided to build a local church. And so, another church was established in another outpost for preaching the gospel—this one in Nijufa in the Bena Bean area. It became well established. We praise God that by His own sovereign will He inspired this chief to come find us so that we could tell him about the word of God. Amen.

Mason forging across a river in their little jeep to reach a remote village

GOD BLESSES SOLIKI

This is a story about Soliki. Soliki lived in a village not too far from Nijufa. It is on the other side of the river. Soliki was a man who had a very nice garden. He would sell his produce on the main road. Most of the buyers were white men who had larger stores. The produce managers would come along, buy his produce, and take it back to the big town of Goroka. Then they would sell that produce to established stores in Goroka. So Soliki would walk up to the road carrying his produce in a string bag over his head.

The white men thought they were very clever. The white men wanted to take advantage of the villagers and get their money back. The white men would do two things to cheat the villager out of his money. They would encourage them to buy beer and get drunk. And then they taught the villagers how to gamble with cards. But the villagers didn't know how to read the cards. So the white men would read them for him. No matter what they did, the villagers would always lose the card game and forfeit all their profit back to the white men. The villagers would often go home empty handed—no produce and no money. This scam was conducted all the time.

Soliki would come home with no produce and no money. His wife was very disappointed. Every time he would come home drunk and without any money or produce. This went on for quite a long while. One day when he came home, his wife asked him, "Aren't you ever going to stop this and start looking after your family?" He was tired and discouraged, so he lay down on the grass on the little mat that they had. Later he recounted the story to Mason: as he lay down, a vision came to him. In this vision he saw a little boy standing with his hand on a black book and his other hand pointing towards Nijufa. And the little boy said to him, "You must go to Nijufa. You must go to that place."

Soliki did not know what it was all about. But his wife reported that when he stood up after lying on the mat for only about ten minutes, he was totally sober. And he told her, "I must go to Nijufa." So he ran out of the hut. He crossed the river and went to Nijufa. He found the chief and he said to him, "I'm looking for a man that has a little book." That was a very unusual thing for them to have there. The chief told him, "Only one man would have a book like that. That man would be the pastor."

So Soliki found the pastor and he said to him, "I don't know what's happening. I came home full of beer and drunk. I lay down. Then I woke up soon after that with a vision to come over here and find a man who has a black book. Maybe you can tell me what it is all about." And the pastor responded, "Yes I can tell you what it's about. God wants you to give up this way of life you are living. He wants you to look after your family. He wants you to bring your money back home. And he wants you to help your wife and your children. God knew that if you would come to me, I would be able to tell you about Him and about His saving grace. I would tell you about His Son, Jesus Christ, and that Jesus loves you and gave His life for you."

Soliki listened very carefully; he realized that the vision meant something very strong and powerful in his life. He asked the pastor, "What can I do?" The pastor answered, "You can open up your heart and receive the Lord Jesus Christ into your heart. I'll help you do that." So he read many scriptures to him from the Word of God and encouraged him to open up his heart and receive the Lord Jesus Christ. The pastor encouraged him to give up his life of drinking. The pastor encouraged him to sell his produce and bring his money back to his family and his wife. So Soliki received Jesus into his heart and became very happy.

And Soliki went back across the river to his village and to his home. He continued to work in his garden. His wife worked with him, and they would take the sweet potato and vegetables to market. They even started growing regular potatoes, Irish potatoes. They didn't eat Irish potatoes very much but they knew the white man liked them. Soliki took those to the road and sold them as well. He told the man that would buy from him, "I don't want any beer. I don't want to gamble." He told the man, "I want to take my money back to my family," which he was able to do. So he brought his money back to his family. Then he decided that he was tired of walking all the way out to the road and became inspired to build a little store where he could sell his produce closer to his village. So he built a little store. And with the money that he was keeping and saving, he was able to open his own trade store. His trade store became a huge success and business people were buying from him all the time.

People began to come and ask him, "What happened to you? Why do you have such a changed life? Why are you living different than you lived before?" Soliki was able to tell them that he had received Jesus Christ in his heart and he was now a Christian living for the Lord. He told them that Jesus helped him to change his life. Then he would tell them, "You can change your life too. Jesus can change you if you will just open up your heart to Him." Because of this simple witness, many people were converted to Christianity. This went on for some time until he had so many people who had received the Lord as their Savior, that he went out beside his house and cleared off some land and he built a little church. Soliki started a church where people could not only come to buy produce from him but they would also come and hear the Word of God.

First of all, God sovereignly spoke to a chief in Nijufa. Secondly, God sovereignly spoke to Soliki to go to Nijufa to hear His Word. Thirdly, Soliki established his own church where people came to hear the Word of God. And lastly, the family was blessed beyond measure with both friends and prosperity. This is one of those true stories where the family actually did live happily ever after. When we last saw Soliki, he was doing a wonderful job of raising his family and witnessing for the Lord and bringing produce for the people. His garden grew so large that he was able to provide a variety of vegetables for many people to purchase. Soliki turned into a wonderful man of God.

ANNANISO TAUGHT TO READ

This is the story about Annaniso. Annaniso was one of the ladies at Kapakamarigi that led a ladies group within our Foursquare church. We also had a thriving daily Bible study program operating out of Kapakamarigi. We didn't have the Pidgin Bible for many years, but the Lutheran mission organization partnered with others, including us, to write what we thought was a suitable translation. We started with the Book of John. Then we translated other books of the Bible as time permitted. A limited Pidgin Bible finally came to be, but there were but a few that could read it. We started a new literacy course to teach our young pastors how to read so that they could take advantage of this new publication. We still encouraged them to memorize the Bible stories we shared, but now we could teach and train our pastors to read.

We were not teaching the ladies, for we had only enough staff to teach the pastors. And so Annaniso was sitting there listening to the pastor preach and teach. She often thought that it would be nice if she knew how to read, and she wished she knew how to read. While she was thinking that, she felt in her heart that the Lord said, "I will teach you." And she thought, "Oh! That would be wonderful if You would teach me to read!"

Most of the children in school had already learned how to read, including Annaniso's son. So she borrowed his Bible, went outside, sat down, and opened the Bible. She had never read before but she began to read. God sovereignly taught Annaniso how to read. God taught Annaniso how to read His Word. Since

God taught her how to read, she would carry the Bible with her everywhere she went. She read the Bible to those who couldn't read it. She became an outstanding teacher; and she used that which God had given to her, the ability to read, to help other people. Annaniso blossomed into a godly woman, sharing her miracle and reading His Word to whoever needed to hear!

JOESO AND KOTOLO AT MAREKAPATO

This is a story about a young couple at Marekapato. Their names are Joeso and Kotolo. Joeso had a very bad sore on his leg near his hip. This often happens in the tropics of Papua New Guinea. When they scratch it, it becomes infected and begins to spread and ultimately becomes ulcerated. We have had those kinds of sores often and do not like dealing with them. Joeso was not familiar with the Foursquare church, so he did not come down to the mission station. As his sore worsened to the point that he couldn't walk, all he could do was lie down on the grass in his hut. Kotolo, his wife, said, "I will go to the garden and get some fresh sweet potato and come back and fix you something to eat. Maybe that will help you feel better." So off she went to the garden.

We had a Foursquare church right near this village. Kotolo could go to the garden by four different paths; all four of them led to the garden. But on this day, she felt she should take a new path that she had never taken before. It "happened" to be the path that went right in front of the Foursquare church. And it also "happened" to be, just as she was in front of the church, that she heard the pastor say to the people, "If anyone is sick today we are going to do something different. Normally I always pray for you, but I want you to know that you can pray for each other and God will hear your prayer. All you have to do, according to the Word of God, is to lay your hands on the sick and they will recover. So we are going to have you to do that this morning." And as the sick people began to raise their hands, others began to go over to lay their hands upon them.

As Kotolo heard and saw this through the window, she thought, "I have a sick husband at home. Maybe if I go lay my hands on him he will be healed." So she quickly turned around and went back to her husband, who was almost asleep at that time. She wakened him and said, "I know how to make you well real quick." And he said, "Oh, you are not a witch doctor. Go to the garden and get the sweet potato." And she said, "No, no! I know how to make you well real quick." He said, "Get out of here before I hit you." And that would've been normal; because when a woman did not obey her husband, their custom was to pick up anything and throw it at her. But before she left, she quickly put her hand on her husband and asked that this Jesus these people were talking about would heal her husband. And she turned and ran out of the hut and off to the garden.

She was gone most of the day digging in the garden. Their sweet potato grows on little mounds that are made in the garden. They would dig in the bottom of that mound and take out the ripe sweet potatoes and then cover it up again and let the rest of the potatoes grow to large sizes. They had no way to preserve food, so they had to go every day and take only what they were going to eat that day. Kotolo had this large bag of sweet potatoes over her head hanging down her back. Bent over with such a heavy load, she trudged home.

She came to her village and climbed over the side of the bamboo ladder to get to her hut. She immediately noticed a young man playing with her children. And as she looked at this young man, she thought, "I know that young man. That's my husband!" About that time he also saw her and came running towards her. His first words were, "How did you learn to do that?" She asked him, "Do what?" He held out his leg. "Look at my leg." She looked at his leg and saw that the sore was completely gone. He was healed from the prayer of an unbeliever. Can you imagine that! She was not totally an unbeliever because she really did believe in her heart that what she heard that pastor say would work. She told her husband, "Well, I just did what the man in that church down there said to do." He said, "Well, let's go talk to him."

So they walked down to the church together and told this story to the pastor of the church. He prayed with them and asked them if they would like to receive the Man who had healed him. They responded, "Yes, we certainly would." So Joeso and Kotolo received the Lord Jesus Christ into their hearts that day and became believers. They also became members of the church in the village of Marekapato. What a wonderful story! Jesus does hear prayer.

Some people say God doesn't direct the paths of unbelievers or answer an unbeliever's prayer. We say, "Well, God must not have read all the theological books or the philosophical and doctrinal posits on faith; so He doesn't know that He can't do that." God can do all things. He is a sovereign God. And He certainly does hear the sinner's prayer or else we would all be unsaved. We were all sinners and we all have sinned and come short of the glory of God (Rom. 3:23). We thank God for Jesus who died on the cross to take away the sins of the world (John 1:29). Anyone who believes in Him and calls upon the name of the Lord shall be saved (Rom. 10:13).

Chapter 13
"FEAR NOT, FOR I AM WITH YOU"

*Fear not, for I am with you; Be not dismayed, for I
am your God. I will strengthen you, Yes, I will help
you, I will uphold you with My righteous right hand.*
—ISAIAH 41:10

FTER THE COUNTRY of Papua New Guinea received its
independence in 1975, many foreign ideas, materials,
publications, movies, and newspaper from the modern
Western world penetrated the culture. Prior to their independence, Australia governed what was allowed to be imported into
the country and prohibited contraband materials, publications,
movies, newspaper, and anything else that would promote nega-
tive cultural values. The newly elected government of Papua New
Guinea, taking the lead from most of the mission schools developed by missionaries, began to open secular elementary, primary,
and high schools. The children and young people were receiving
public education, and they would graduate from high school and
college, but they had no employment opportunity.

This influx of Western media promoted the Western mindset.
The young people would see how the white man was living in the
movies, the videos, the fictional stories in magazines, and they
wanted to live like that. They wanted to have those same possessions. They wanted money to purchase the things they saw in
the movies, the newspapers, and the magazines; but they had no
way to earn money because the government had no employment

agency to transition graduates into jobs. So the young people, fresh out of high school, would form "rascal gangs." In reality, we would call them criminals by any Western standard; but the government of Papua New Guinea, because they were very young people and normally just out of high school, decided to call them "rascals." So they became commonly known as "rascal gangs." These rascal gangs were armed and dangerous. They began to hijack cars along the road. They would steal from homes. They would stop trucks under the guise of a toll and rob the drivers of their cargo. Or when the trucks were slowly climbing steep mountain passes, the rascals would jump onto the bed of the truck, cut the tarp open, and steal the cargo. Sometimes they would rape women. Sometimes they would even kill, depending on their state of mind and just how much they had given themselves over to the influence of the devil. The rascal gangs had infested our area, and it soon became very dangerous to travel anywhere.

Thirty Bullets Holes

A rascal gang had taken up residence in a village nearby one of our churches. They would constantly be seen menacing the people and destroying the area. So the pastor of the village church ventured into their stronghold and convinced them to let him talk to them. They were not too happy about the presence of the pastor. The pastor began to tell them about Jesus and the power of God and the love of God and how that God loved them. He also told them what they were doing to people was wrong. He told them that the things they were doing would actually lead them to being arrested and put into jail if they were caught.

It was very difficult to catch these rascal gangs because they were able to flee into the jungle bushes and into the trees and the high grass. If the police did come, they came outfitted with heavy tactical boots and other protective and defensive equipment that caused them to be clumsy and move slowly. They could not move around as quickly as the rascals because of all their gear. The barefoot rascals were unencumbered, so they could flee quickly and get away easily. Villagers were afraid to report the rascal gangs to the authorities because of the payback system. If anyone reported them, then the rascal gang would pay them back by harming that person who reported and menacing their family and friends. So they ran their business and gang activities pretty free of any interference from the villagers or authorities.

They didn't like the pastor coming and telling them that what they were doing was wrong. They weren't impressed with his story that God loves them, they could have a better life, and there is a God in heaven who wanted to help them. They decided to reject this pastor and his message. So they began a rumor around the village that they were going to kill the pastor when he came home. The rascal gang prepared to kill this pastor. The people who heard this rumor came and told the pastor. They told him, "They are going to hide along the trail you take to go home. They said they are going to kill you." The pastor was not afraid; he knew God was with him. To protect his family, he decided that he would send his wife and children on ahead, separate from him. He sent them on home up the trail. He started up the trail himself a little later on.

These rascal gangs had robbed many homes, private citizens, and stores and had accumulated pistols and rifles that they used. So the rascal gang went up on the trail and hid themselves waiting for the pastor. When the pastor came around a bend in the trail, the rascal gang stormed him and began to shoot at him with their pistols and rifles. The pastor kept on walking. They kept shooting. He kept walking. They had never seen anything like that! They were accustomed to provoking fear. They had never seen anyone keep walking so calmly while they were shooting. They emptied their pistols and rifles into that pastor, and he still kept on walking. Fear came upon the rascals. They quickly threw their guns away and ran down the hill and went back to their village.

The pastor continued on to his home where his wife was waiting. When he arrived home, he changed his shirt. His wife picked up the shirt he was wearing and counted thirty bullet holes in his shirt. Not one bullet from any rifle or pistol had pierced his skin. That is the power of God! God said, "Lo, I am with you always" (Matt. 28:20). And He certainly was with this pastor. This pastor was there to do something good in the name of God and to try and help this rascal gang. Jesus was there also. The pastor was going as commanded—to go into all the world, to go into every village and preach the gospel (Mark 16:15). He was doing what God told him to do. And God was there to help him and certainly to be with him.

About two months later, Mason decided to go down to visit this place because he heard a rumor that the rascal gang had, because of this miracle, received Jesus Christ into their hearts. We traveled to this stronghold village where the rascal gang was holed up. To our amazement, when we got there we saw a building. A nice big building had been built; it was a church. And the village was having church services there. We discovered that the leader of the rascal gang and all his gang were the leadership of that church. They had cut bamboos and fashioned them into drums, they had a guitar, and they were playing and singing praise and worship songs. They invited Mason to speak to them.

That entire rascal gang had received Jesus, built a church, and the entire village was participating in services. We had a wonderful time praying for the sick and seeing the sick healed. We prayed for the baptism of the Holy Spirit. They received the Holy Spirit. Seeing this rascal gang come out of darkness into the light of the glorious Son of God and serve Jesus with all their hearts was an amazing blessing (1 Pet. 2:9). They used to serve themselves through robbing and stealing. Now they were serving God through praise and worship. God is powerful. We did not hear about this type of miracle too often. But God can do all things. Nothing is impossible with God (Luke 1:37).

Local Leaders now pastoring their own church service

FIGHT IN THE ROAD

There were many times the Lord looked after us, especially when driving along the beat-up dirt roads. On this occasion we happened upon a fight in the road. Our family was going to Goroka from Lae. We were coming around the bend in the road just south of Henganofi when we saw large crowds of people, mainly warrior men, right in the middle of the road. They were all in a knock-down, drag-out violent fight. One man was backing down the road with his arms raised above his head. He had a big rock in his hands and was proceeding to pound another person. He didn't hear the car because of all the commotion and all the yelling and the fighting. He had no clue that we were coming. We saw him and the violent crowd just as we came around the bend. Mason stomped the brakes really hard. By the time we stopped, this man was right in front of our vehicle. His back was to us, but we were afraid that he might turn around and throw the rock right at us. Virgene had just enough time to shout, "Jesus! Jesus!" as she called upon the name of Jesus for protection. You don't always have time to pray, but you can always call out to Jesus. He is the One who saves!

The man stepped back and into the vehicle, turned around quickly and saw us, dropped the rock on the ground, and proceeded over to the side of the road. His rage was gone. He looked calm. He appeared to be in a trance. The others saw our vehicle, and they all stepped over to the side of the road in such a polite and friendly way. We were dumbfounded. This violent crowd of fighting villagers became docile enough to let us pass. Did they see something we did not see? Are angels that awesome? The hands of God parted that violent crowd so we could pass unharmed. We drove right on through and continued our trip to Henganofi on the way to Goroka. We stopped at the patrol officer headquarters in Henganofi and told him about the fight going on down the road. We cautioned him and asked that he might go have a look so as to prevent a riot. That is what he did.

We went on to Goroka and conducted our business that we had to do there. The next day, on our return trip, we stopped in to say hello to the patrol officer. We always stopped in to greet the folks we met while traveling because they were often the only people to talk with along the road. So we stopped again at Henganofi to say hello to the patrol officer. He told us, "I'm glad you came and told me about the fight on the road. When I got there, one man had already been stoned. He was killed with rocks that they were throwing at each other." He went on to tell us that he managed to stop the fighting and got them to return to their own villages. So that's another time when the Lord protected us. They could have just thrown the rock right at us. In their anger, they could have attacked us, but the Lord caused them to cease being violent for the moment, step aside, and let us pass peacefully without being harmed. The Lord was certainly with us.

THE THIEF STEALS PEANUTS

This is a story of a peanut factory worker. Her name is Salie. Salie had worked at the peanut factory for quite a long time. She also came to our church. To use the word *factory* sounds like a big enterprise; but it was just a small little store in a one-room building that they used to clean, shell, and bag the peanuts to take them to market. Salie was a faithful employee. She told us this story.

The peanut factory was broken into and the thieves stole a lot of peanuts. So she was telling her workmates, "You know, that reminds me of a story in the Bible. I'm a Christian; and the Bible says that Jesus is coming back again like a thief in the night. And because we were not prepared and ready, the thief broke in and he stole from our factory. So you must be ready at all times because Jesus is coming back. He will come back just like a thief in the night." There were four other girls in the room. They were concerned, "If that is true, then we are not ready. How do we get ready for Jesus?" So Salie told them how they could get ready. She told them if they confessed with their mouths the Lord Jesus and believed in their hearts that God raised him from the dead, they would be saved (Rom. 10:9). So she led them in prayer and they received the Lord as their Savior. And they were rejoicing. And everything was going great.

But a couple of hours later, a message came to Salie that the boss wanted to see her in his office. And, of course, anyone that has worked in and around a place of business knows that sometimes the boss doesn't want employees to be talking of things that are political or religious in the conduct of daily business. Salie was faced with a choice. Was she going to go in and tell what happened? Or, was she going to go in and just say it was nothing? Salie decided she was going to tell the truth, that she was witnessing to her fellow workers about the Lord. She trusted the Lord would be with her.

So she went in to the see the boss. The first thing the boss said was, "What's this I hear that you've been telling the workers?" She could have said a lot of things, but she told it just like it was. She responded, "Sir, I'm a Christian. And the Bible says that Christ is coming back to receive Christians and take them to be in heaven where He is. But you must be ready because His coming will be like a thief in the night. Remember that you had a thief break into your factory last night, and he stole peanuts because we were not ready for him. So you must be ready for Christ's coming because He's coming just like that." The boss looked at her and said, "Salie, if that's true I don't know how to receive the Lord. I am not ready. How do I get ready for the Lord to come?" So Salie was able to lead her boss to the Lord. Five Christians were born into the kingdom of God because Salie used an opportunity to tell them about the Lord Jesus Christ.

Salie's life was not an easy life. She came to church by herself because her husband refused to come with her. Eventually he got tired of being home by himself. So he told her, "You can't go to church anymore. You have to stay home." But she said, "No! I'm a Christian. I must obey the Lord! I must go to church. I'll be with you all the other days of the week, but I must go to church on Sunday." So she kept coming to church.

He began to threaten her for doing so. One night when she came to church, she shared with us, "Please pray for me when I go home tonight. My husband says he's going to kill me if I go to church again. I've come with that threat on my life." So we all prayed for Salie and she went home with confidence that the Lord would be with her. When we saw her the next day, her arm was in a sling. We asked, "What happened, Salie?" She responded, "Oh, my husband did try to kill me; but all he could do was break my arm. I am going to still serve the Lord even if I cannot come to church right now."

Many, many years later when we were in Papua New Guinea in 2006, we were in the Lae church. A man came up and threw his arms around us and said, "I am Salie's husband. I want to thank you for what you did for my wife. You put the faith and the love of Christ in her heart. Because of her love and her faithfulness, I have received the Lord and I'm serving the Lord. Not only that, but Salie has become a pastor of a church. I'm helping her to pastor. That church is near Bololo." So Salie's faithfulness and trust in the Lord proved true. The Bible says, "Wives, likewise, be submissive to your own husbands, that even if some do not obey the word, they, without a word, may be won by the conduct of their wives" (1 Pet. 3:1). So thank you, Salie, for what you've done and for the blessings that others have received from the Lord because of your faithfulness.

THREE LITTLE PIGS

This is a story of the three pigs. Right near our village there was a lady that had three pigs. All the ladies raise a certain amount of pigs. They love their pigs. Pigs symbolize wealth and social status. The more pigs a family has, the wealthier they are. The New Guineans treat their pigs almost like children. Accidentally running over a stray pig in the middle of the road is a major crime in Papua New Guinea to this day. Baby pigs are often taken away from their mother and nursed by the ladies in the village. They will admit that they cherish these pigs because they are of great value.

One morning the lady went out to feed her pigs and found that one was missing. This became a great crisis and a cause for concern for her. She was afraid she had lost him. She didn't know what to do. And she said, "My pig has wandered away and I hope it will come back." So after two days when it had not come back, she was telling one of her friends about how sad she was at the loss of her pig. This friend of hers was a Christian. This friend had learned that you could trust God with everything, even all of your belongings—your wealth or your goods and even with your animals and your pigs. Her friend knew that you can trust God with your whole life because God is concerned about all of you, your things, and your entire welfare.

So she said to this lady, "Have you prayed about it?" This lady was a Christian too, but she responded, "No, I did not know that Jesus would be concerned about my pig." Her friend encouraged her, "Oh yes, Jesus loves you and He loves all that you have. Jesus said ask what you will and it shall be done for you" (John 15:7). So they knelt together and they prayed that the Lord would bring this pig back. The next day when she opened the door to go out to feed her two pigs, there was the third. God had brought that pig back. Where it was or what it had been doing, no one knows—but God. God was with that lady; He heard and answered that prayer for a woman in Papua New Guinea who prayed. God answered her prayer and brought her pig back and restored it to her again.

SLEEP IN PEACE

One day when Mason was at a village ministering, he was preparing to leave and a dear lady about forty to forty-five years of age came and stood in front of him. She pointed her stubby fingers at him (her fingers were just stubs due to the common traditional practice among the natives of cutting off a joint of a finger when someone dies). She spoke to Mason, "When you go back to the people who sent you to tell us about Jesus, would you thank them for me? Because before you came I was not able to go in my house and sleep. I would go out and sleep among the rocks and the trees and hide in the bushes and take my family with me. We were afraid the enemy would come and set fire to the house and shoot us. We would go outdoors because we lived in fear and had to hide ourselves. But you came and you told us about Jesus. I have Jesus in my heart now. Now I can go into my house and sleep at night with peace because Jesus has given me peace."

She did not know the Bible. But Psalm 4:8 tells us, "I will both lie down in peace, and sleep; For You alone, O Lord, make me dwell in safety." She was enjoying the promises of God because she has the true living God and His living Word within her heart. The Word was helping her to live out a fearless life. She had lived in fear, now she was living in peace because the Prince of Peace was now living in her heart and she knew He was with her.

Chapter 14
REFLECTIONS

Give thanks to the Lord and proclaim his great-
ness. Let the whole world know what he has
done....Remember the wonders he has performed,
his miracles, and the rulings he has given.
—1 CHRONICLES 16:8, 12, NIV

A s WE LOOK back at the years we spent in Papua New Guinea, the land to which and the people to whom the Lord brought us, it is a marvel to behold what God has done. The gospel of the Lord Jesus Christ began cleaning up the people inside and out. With no prompting from us but only in response to the Holy Spirit, one of the first things these natives who had never had a bath wanted to do when they became Christians was to clean themselves. And then they wanted clothes to cover their nakedness. As they relinquished their man-killing arrows and all they represented, they instead embraced the love and compassion of Christ and extended that to their fellow man—even their former enemies.

They saw a new way of life and wanted to learn those new things. They asked for schools. Many of the children who came into the mission station at an early age were able to rise from their centuries-old culture to become high school graduates. We felt that it was important to provide as many schools as we could for the children in the villages who were not able to come to the mission station. We started primary schools in the villages.

Classes were conducted in Pidgin to try and reach those who were missing out on education. We wanted them to be able to read the Bible and other literature in Pidgin. We felt this would make them better citizens. We also conducted schools in different areas to teach prospective Bible students to read and write in Pidgin. These were geared to ages fifteen years and older.

We were interested in all aspects of the lives of "our people." We sought the Lord on ways to improve the lives of the women in that culture. We taught them concepts of sanitation and health care. We introduced them to new foods or better varieties. In time groups were organized where the women learned to sew and knit. As they came together for these meetings, they enjoyed the fellowship of other Christian women. All of these things provided a sense of achievement and accomplishment that they could better provide for their families.

Of primary importance, of course, was the peace of both mind and heart that came to those who accepted Christ as Savior and Lord. We watched these people who had been held captive for centuries by the witch doctors through fear and superstition come to a saving knowledge of the Lord Jesus Christ and embrace the freedom He gives. There are thousands who have been liberated from fear and death and despair. There are thousands who can now gladly testify to the mighty transforming power of God in their lives and rejoice in the joy and peace available in Him. There are thousands who will populate heaven because of the ministry we were privileged to be a part of. There are thousands who have put down their arrows of war and taken up the torch of God to share the good news of Jesus Christ with their countrymen and on into the world beyond. We were in the right place at the right time for God to use us to help turn a people and a nation toward Him. Those twenty-three years we gave to His service to these people was a wonderful investment we feel honored to have made.

We Gave Them Our All

At one of our farewell celebrations we experienced the largest *mumu* (cooking food in a hole in the ground) we had ever seen. A very old man made his way over to Mason and looked him in the face. With tears in his eyes, he spoke to Mason slowly and intentionally, "When you first came to my country you had black hair and it was very thick. Now you are leaving my country and your hair is white and thin. This shows me that you have given all your strength to my people and my country. I want to thank you for that."

Celebrating Fifty Years

In July 2006 the native leaders of PNG Foursquare church led by Timothy Tipitap planned to celebrate fifty years since we came sharing the gospel of Jesus Christ in the Eastern Highlands of PNG. They invited all of our family to attend. They invited Mason to be one of the guest speakers along with Dr. Jack Hayford, at that time president of the International Church of the Foursquare Gospel. All five of our children and some of their spouses and families were there also. This was such a blessing, for some of our children had not been back for twenty-five years or more. How excited we all were!

Jack Hayford and the Hughes family at the fiftieth anniversary of the Foursquare work in PNG in 2006 (left to right—back row: Kay Hughes, Hal Abner, Bruce Hughes, Brittani Hughes-Carpenter, Gordon Booth, Sondra Hughes-Booth; middle row: Nicole Abner, Natasha Abner, Denise Hughes-Abner, Jack Hayford, Michele Hughes-Burum, Stephanie Hughes-Stimpert; front row: Brandi Hughes, Mason Hughes, and Virgene Hughes)

For the opening on the first day, a march for Jesus was made through the town of Goroka, with several hundred marching. It was led by the local police. The men wore ties and caps in the Foursquare colors. The women wore wraparound skirts and blouses of the same colors that they had made, and they carried umbrellas that matched. The march ended at the soccer field— where the celebration was held, since Goroka did not have a large enough building to accommodate the large crowd. It was estimated there were 20,000 people in attendance.

At the meeting that first night, everyone was given a three-inch piece of candle as they arrived. Later in the service they called Mason and Virgene to the front of the platform and lit our two candles. Then they had us to walk down the first row of people to light two of their candles. They in turn lit two others' candles, and those two lit someone near to them. Soon the whole soccer field was alight with candles, giving an amazing visual to signify how the gospel had spread throughout PNG. What a glorious sight!

After the convention our whole family went to Dunantina Valley to the Hageri Mission Station to see the timber house we had made of pit sawn timber, where our children had grown up. It was still in good shape; the local pastor was living in it. What a thrill for our kids to see their childhood home, the river where they swam every day, and some of their friends they played with as children! This was such a wonderful blessing for all of us!

OVERVIEW OF THE FOURSQUARE WORK IN PAPUA NEW GUINEA 1956–1979

But what does it say? "The word is near you, in your mouth and in your heart" (that is, the word of faith which we preach): that if you confess with your mouth the Lord Jesus and believe in your heart that God has raised Him from the dead, you will be saved. For with the heart one believes unto righteousness, and with the mouth confession is made unto salvation. For the Scripture says, "Whoever believes on Him will not be put to shame." For there is no distinction between Jew and Greek, for the same Lord over all is rich to all who call upon Him. For "whoever calls on the name of the Lord shall be saved." How then shall they call on Him in whom they have not believed? And how shall they believe in Him of whom they have not heard? And how shall they hear without a preacher? And how shall they preach unless they are sent? As it is written: "How beautiful are the feet of those who preach the gospel of peace, Who bring glad tidings of good things!"
—ROMANS 10:8–15

WHEN WE LEFT the U.S. with our three children and sailed on the Swedish freighter for twenty-three days in July of 1956, out of ignorance we made an agreement that we would be "spiritual" missionaries, not medical or teaching or building or any of the other types of missionaries of which we had heard. One thing we did know for sure was that we knew absolutely nothing about the people of New Guinea, except that they were primitive.

At the end of our ocean voyage, we landed in Sydney, Australia, where we stayed for six weeks ministering in the Foursquare Bible College. We met Graham and Irene Baker and also Albert and Nell Booth and their three children. Both of these couples were in the Foursquare Bible college and had a burden for missions.

With God's intervention through Ron and Margaret Teale, a guarantee of accommodations had been given to the government of New Guinea so we could get a visa to come into the country. We received permission to enter New Guinea. Ron met us at the airport at Port Moresby. We stayed there with the Teales for the first six weeks. During this time Mason took a few plane trips to the Highlands (there were no roads) seeking where he could settle our family until we could find God's leading as to where to establish the first Foursquare mission station in New Guinea.

Mason visited the gold mining town of Wau, where he was able to rent a house for the family. He flew back to Port Moresby and brought our family to Wau, a small town with some one hundred white people, a post office, and two stores with one small room each. There we began to pray and asked for God's leading.

We found that no English was spoken among the New Guineans. Most only spoke their tribal languages, of which there were 750. We were encouraged to learn New Guinea Pidgin (Pidgin) as some could speak it. So, very quickly we hired a young New Guinean to come in several times a week to help us learn this language. He spoke no English and Pidgin was not written, so we would hold up an object or make a gesture and write down what we thought the young man said. When Mason thought he knew enough of the language, he wrote down a message and got permission from the expatriate gold mine manager to have services on Sunday mornings. Meanwhile Virgene taught Sunday school (with a full gospel message) at the local Anglican church.

In April 1957 the Sydney churches had appointed Albert and Nell Booth to be their first missionaries to New Guinea. They joined us in Wau, renting a house there also, along with their three children, Eileen, Gordon, and Mark. Then Albert felt God leading him on to the Sepik area. He flew to Angoram and found accommodations. His family then joined him there.

After some weeks Mason made arrangements to make an eighteen-day trek through the jungle with several carriers to guide him. He prayed as he went asking God, "Is this the place where you would have us to tell the people about You?" Although he saw many places and had many experiences on that journey, he did not find the place where God would have him. Continuing his search, Mason hitchhiked on fuel trucks, rode up and down the one and only road with other missionaries, and took flights further up in the Highlands scouting out the land. But God had still not yet spoken to him.

After several months Mason saw an advertisement on the bulletin board at the post office for a Jeep for sale by a lady who was returning to Australia. Mason checked over the Jeep and found it in good shape—other than some bullet holes from World War II! He bought it, making travel much easier.

DUNANTINA VALLEY

On one of Mason's trips higher up into the mountains, he met Ross Johnson, a government patrol officer, who invited him to go with him on a patrol up the Dunantina and Kamantina valleys. Mason prayed for guidance. While going up the Dunantina Valley, Ross made one of his routine stops to meet with the people. As Mason looked over the area, God spoke, "This is where I want you to start the mission station." What excitement and gratitude filled his soul! The owner was there and agreed that he would let Mason use the land for a missions station. There was a small hut across the road occasionally used by the government patrol officers; Ross agreed to allow Mason and his family to live there until a proper home could be built after the lease was obtained.

Ross immediately began the procedure required to acquire the government lease for the land. It took nearly a year as the process unfolded, including a notice placed in the *Government Gazette* to make sure no one else wanted it, meetings with the locals, and determination made if in the next ninety-nine years the people would need that piece of land for their population growth. Ninety-nine years was the length of the government lease. But Mason was not concerned, for the Lord had spoken clearly to him. He knew this would be a Foursquare missions station. (At that time the local people were not allowed into the town of Goroka from 6:00 p.m. to 6:00 a.m., so that's why the choice of the village area rather than the town was made for where to establish the Foursquare mission station.) Mason drove back down the mountain to give the family the exciting news.

Not long after that Mason drove back to the Dunantina Valley with a few things in a trailer that the family had managed to buy. He arrived safely at Hageri (which means "salt"), the name of the five acres for which we had applied. He met with the local men (one of those men was Kiabe, a young man who had spent two years on the coast and had learned New Guinea Pidgin and who Mason soon engaged as an interpreter) and asked them to enlarge the one-room patrol house that Ross had said we could use. This mission accomplished, he left the Jeep and trailer in Goroka—only thirty-two miles but a three-hour drive away—and he flew back to Wau. There was a lot of excitement in the Hughes' home.

It was November 1957 that Mason chartered a DC-3 plane to fly our things from Wau to Goroka. At last we arrived. Local men were available to help Mason to load the trailer. We also loaded the two older kids, the dog, the cat, and a duck we had been given in the back of the open-air Jeep. With Virgene and the baby in the front with Mason, we began our three-hour drive.

After turning off the main road, we began the five-mile drive up the Dunantina Valley. There had been a big rain the night before and also that day; so as we started up one very steep hill, the Jeep began to spin and slide. After several tries Mason realized the load was too heavy for the Jeep to pull up the hill. He asked Virgene to stay with the children while he unhooked the trailer, put a few things into the Jeep, and went on up the hill to unload, a trip of less than half an hour.

Virgene and the children found a big rock where they sat as they watched the Jeep disappear over the hill. The Jeep was just out of sight when men, who did not appear very friendly and were dressed only in loin cloths and feathered headdresses and holding bows and arrows, surrounded the rock. Virgene's heart sank; they were, she knew, in an area where they practiced cannibalism. As she prayed, she felt the Lord tell her to smile at the men. After a short while the natives began to smile in response.

Even so, it was a wonderful relief when the Jeep came back over the hill.

Kiabe returned with Mason and quickly found out that the men were a hunting party. He engaged them in helping to hook the trailer onto the now empty Jeep and get it back on the road. We loaded our family and off we went up the hill to our new bush home. Thus life began for the Hughes family in the Dunantina Valley, 5,500 feet up in the mountains.

Mason hired Kiabe to help around the house, cut firewood, make a fire in the woodstove, etc., as well as be our interpreter. Kiabe was his native name; but Mason had trouble remembering that name, so he named him Sam. In the valley of 25,000 people, there were only two people who could speak the New Guinea Pidgin, the language that we had learned. So Sam was our right-hand man to interpret anytime the people wanted to talk to us. Sam was our very first convert; we knew he must know Jesus before he could properly interpret the message of the gospel. He was a real treasure. He stayed with us the whole twenty three years.

The people surrounded our home day after day peering in the shutter windows, as they had never seen anything like us and the way we lived before. Within a very short time, Mason started to have Sunday services on the side of the hill in our yard with everyone sitting or squatting on the ground. Each week the numbers grew.

We began to look at the natives with their scabies, boils, and burns and listen to them tell about their malaria, pneumonia, dysentery, etc. We remembered the policy we had set on the boat of only ministering to their "spiritual" needs; but how could we say no to such a needy people? Our hearts went out to these people we had grown to love. So Mason started treating their physical needs as well as telling them about Jesus. Soon the government hospital began to give us medical supplies.

After the New Year, it was time for Stephanie to start school. Mason made a desk for her and Virgene began to teach her. We made a policy that the natives could not stand at the windows or door and talk while Stephanie was in school. The curious natives wondered what Virgene was doing. When it was explained to them about reading and writing, they asked Mason to build a school and teach their children to read and write. We were beginning to learn that being "spiritual" missionaries included living our lives as examples and showing the love of Jesus to these people in many practical ways.

Mason began to minister in other villages up and down the valley and over the many mountain ranges in addition to the Sunday services at the house. Virgene had also started a Sunday school. We were soon going to have our fourth child, an addition that we were all happy about.

After six long months of ministering, Mason had his first village convert. What a thrill this was! The man, Tabiak, came to the door after service wanting some clothes. He also made a motion with his fingers, which we finally understood to mean that he wanted scissors because he had seen Virgene cutting the family's hair. The next day we saw a man squatting among other people on the lawn. He was clean, had his hair cut and washed, and had clothes on. Mason asked Sam who the visitor was. Sam laughed and told us it was Tabiak. What a joy and transformation—first inside, then outside!

In early May we had our first overseas visitor, Dr. Harold Chalfant, from the Foursquare Missions Department in Los Angeles. He loved the people and took many pictures. Just ten days after he left, Virgene woke up early and told Mason she needed to start the long trip to the Goroka hospital. Mason loaded everyone into the Jeep and took off for Goroka. On May 16 our Michele Irene was born at 5 pounds 10 ounces. When we brought her home, people walked miles and hours over mountain ranges to see the tiny blonde white baby.

THE WORK EXPANDS

The work began to grow as more and more chiefs would come and request Mason to come to their villages and tell their people about the "Man" who had power over the witch doctor. Soon Mason was walking into many areas and over many mountains, often spending the night, to reach the people who were hungry to hear about this Man Jesus.

A few weeks later we had a letter from Albert Booth saying that he would like to come and visit us. Mason went to town to meet the plane in our Willys Jeep truck that Foursquare Missions had sent us from the U.S. How proud of that we were! We no longer had to ride in the open air; a great blessing, especially in the rainy season.

The mission work was expanding and was now almost more than Mason could handle. Albert wanted to come back and bring his family and work near us. This was an answer to prayer, as the Imaka area (a five-hour drive from us) was crying out for a missionary. Albert was able to buy our old blue Jeep for his family. The Booths also lived in a native-style house. Immediately the work began to grow under their ministry. (Their son Gordon and our daughter Sondra then grew up together. They were married in Swansea, Australia, in 1973.)

Soon after that we received the wonderful news that our mission lease had been granted. This was an answer to prayer as it was the rainy season and Michele had already had pneumonia twice from living in the damp bush house. Mason had faith that it would happen, and so he already had several teams sawing boards with pit saws to build our timber house, as there was no sawmill in the area. After moving onto the mission lease land, we found why the people had released this piece of land for us to have. It had been a former fighting ground, and no one wanted to live there because of all the spirits of the dead walking around. But this did not bother us. This was God's holy ground.

When the house was complete enough for us to move into, then Mason started building the church. By the time it was built, it was much too small so we still had to meet outside. By now 1,000 villagers were attending. Then Mason began training "Leader Boys" to have services in their own villages. This helped reduce the church attendance somewhat. By now Mason was having services in many, many villages and areas. Then the demand for a school became evident, so a school building had to be built out of the bush material. We used galvanized iron for the roof, as it helped to funnel rain water into our 1,000 gallon water tanks to sustain us through the six-month dry season.

We set up both a Bible school and Christian day school at Hageri, which provided a constant source of native pastors and workers. Preaching of the gospel was always our first priority. About three years after establishing the work at Hageri, on Sundays when Virgene held services, Mason would hike endless miles through the jungle and over the mountain to reach other villages. We also either did the work ourselves or oversaw the preparation and construction of the mission station and all that entailed, including all the buildings and landscaping. We carried a very heavy work schedule. Soon Mason was taking care of medical needs, teaching classes in the day school, preaching each

Sunday, running the five-acre missions station, and ministering in all the outlying areas.

Mason had to go to Goroka every ten days or so for supplies. Virgene and the children went only about every six weeks or so. It was a wonderful break and always a special time of fellowship that we treasured. Also, our time in town gave us opportunity to get acquainted and visit with missionaries from other areas. Because of our busy schedules sometimes it was the only time we could spend time with them. This would be the only time we would see another white person unless the patrol officer would drop in for a cup of tea or sometimes when our family and the Booths would visit each other.

The mission work continued to increase. Also, our children were growing, so Virgene was teaching the older three children by correspondence from a course supplied by the government of Queensland, Australia. This was in addition to managing the house; baking and sewing clothes for the family; doing all the secretary work, the bookkeeping, and the report work for the mission; and, of course, running and teaching the Sunday school. The strain began to tell on our bodies, and it became evident that we needed a rest. One day in January 1960, as Virgene sat down to type some reports, a great weariness came over her. She turned to Mason and commented, "I am so very tired that I can't make my fingers work." "Well, why don't you go to bed and get some rest," he responded. She did go to bed and remained there three months. Even after that length of time her strength was not fully restored.

A young male nurse from the Foursquare church of Perth, Western Australia, came to visit us and expressed his burden for missions. Ian Van Zuilecom had been working with the government in New Guinea for several years and wanted a change.

He joined with us. This was a real burden lifted, as Ian immediately took over the medical work for Mason. Also, the school was now in its second year and there was a need for a second teacher. Ian also filled this slot. Ian was a man of extraordinary abilities; within a few months he was able to take over the management of the school and mission station. That afforded us the freedom to return to America for a furlough.

When we returned to the United States on our first furlough in July of 1960, we left behind nine established churches. Because of the pool of infectious diseases in the Highlands and among the people and in spite of our diligent care in cooking and every area of hygiene, our whole family was in need of medical attention when we returned to the States. Although most of us responded to care and recovered quickly, it was many months before Virgene's health fully returned. By God's grace and healing power, when the furlough was over, we were all enjoying good health again.

While we were gone, Ian looked after the mission and Ray and Tryph Pearson and their daughter, Ruth, were sent from Perth to help him. The work continued to grow and increase. That year was the first outpouring of the Holy Spirit. We had met Rev. Leo Harris who had a large church in Adelaide, South Australia, called Christian Revival Crusade (CRC). He was very impressed by the young couple who would give their lives for missions. He contacted Ian and Bob Tracy, missionaries in Perth, Australia. A working agreement was made for their organization to send missionaries to help with the Foursquare work at Hageri. Five single ladies were sent. Merrilyn Teague and Pauline Kelly had been through our Foursquare Bible College in Perth. Bernice Halley was sent to be the head teacher of the school, which was still growing. Dorothy Kitto was sent to help with the medical work as she was a registered nurse (RN). Helen Evans was sent from Perth. A house was built to accommodate these ladies. Also, Mr. and Mrs. Hann were sent from Adelaide. He was to help with the maintenance of the vehicles and houses.

During this time, the Foursquare Mission Board asked us to go to the Philippines, as Dr. Alan Hamilton had taken ill and had to return to the U.S. The Mission Board felt there were now sufficient missionaries in New Guinea. At that time they placed Rev. Bob Tracy in charge of New Guinea missions. With heavy hearts, yet knowing we were in God's perfect will, we said yes to the Mission Board.

We remained in the Philippines for twenty-six months. Mason was the missions director of this great field of the Philippines and gleaned much knowledge from the experience. He traveled almost constantly to all the islands in addition to his responsibilities as the pastor of the main church and director of the Manila Christian Day School. During this time in Manila, God gave us another beautiful baby girl, Denise Lynne, born May 11, 1963. So, now we had a New Guinean and a Filipino.

Even though we were busy in ministry, our hearts still cried for New Guinea and the people there. The work there was constantly growing; Bob Tracy and the Mission Board informed us they needed a leader on the spot. After what seemed like a very long time away, the Mission Board allowed us to once again return to the country and people for whom we were so burdened.

An outpouring of the Holy Spirit had come in 1963, with the empowerment that is promised in Acts 1:8. The gospel was preached and miracles followed in a greater and more expansive way. This inspired great faith among the people. What a welcome awaited us when we returned in July of 1964 as the school children and people lined the driveway of Hageri! Just a few weeks after we arrived, Dr. McPherson, Dr. Hamilton, and Dr. Edwards from Foursquare came for a visit to see firsthand what God was doing in this primitive country. What a joy they found on the faces of the people who had found Jesus as their Savior! Those who had no god before now loved the God of all gods.

Soon others arrived at the mission station to join forces and others left who had served their terms. Wayne and Jane Bienvenu came; Jane as a teacher and Wayne as a maintenance man. Jim and Elva Schroder also came; Jim as a teacher and Elva as a helper. Wally Lipscomb came from Perth. He was an Anglican priest who had come to know Jesus and came into our church in Perth. He and Ian worked together for a time in the nearby Mendi area. The churches were sending men from Australia to help build homes and churches. The McKernans came to minister, and also Ronda Millard and Yvonne Wilson. Then some single men, Laurie Hall and George Brixey, came. David Kitto helped for a short period of time. Also, Mike and Margaret Dawson came. Margaret helped in the school and Mike helped in maintenance. The teachers and other helpers all desired to go out on weekend ministries. What a time of testimonies we had as we all gathered for a Sunday evening service in our home! One evening in 1964 Mason was excited to share that a lady was raised from the dead in the Kamantina Valley. One evening in 1965, during one of these services, the Holy Spirit gave a prophecy that this group would soon be divided for God's work.

It was only a matter of weeks before two of our single ladies, Pauline Kelly and Helen Evans, came to us and said the Lord had put a burden on their hearts to go to Gotomi, a village in the same district, and open a Pidgin Bible school. This meant walking over mountains for three hours for there was no road.

Soon a house was built for the girls and a school building was erected. The first Foursquare Bible school was opened. What dedication these two young ladies had! Mason had already been going into Gotomi for several months and ministering to the villages there. This area had opened up through a miracle of love shown from Mason to Assistant Chief Baieso after he had stepped off the back of Mason's truck.

A few months later Ray and Tryph Pearson came to Mason saying they felt God leading them to open a church in Kainantu. Mason and Ray went to Kainantu and found the land they felt was right. They asked the government for a lease. Not long after that a church building and home were built for the Pearsons and the church was started in Kainantu. Also, the Kapakamarigi station was opened during these years with a church and homes built there for missionaries and national pastors. The work continued to grow there. We later held our youth camps and conventions there.

Australian Foursquare missionaries Graham and Irene Baker and their family arrived in Port Moresby in the early 1960s. Soon after their arrival they moved to the Highlands to work in the Fore area. After some years they moved to Madang and established a large church and works in other areas.

Mason met several times with the Booths and others from the Foursquare churches in Sydney, Australia, trying to get the two Foursquare missions organizations (Australia and Los Angeles) to become one. The pastors in Sydney area could not come to an agreement with Los Angeles; so there continued to be two Foursquare missions. But that did not hinder very good working relationships among the missionaries, whether Foursquare or other denominations. Later Australia and U.S. did merge into one Foursquare church in PNG.

It was in 1965 that Mason and the other missionaries felt it was time to have a New Guinea convention. All the plans came together and the first Foursquare New Guinea Convention was held at Hageri with some 2,000 people in attendance. What a blessed time it was! Not long after, youth camps were organized, one of the many blessings that came from these gatherings.

One day we received a letter from Laurie Hall and Ronda Millard saying they wanted to get married. They wanted Mason to come to Goroka to perform the wedding on November 14, 1965. Then Laurie and Ronda said they had a burden to go and pastor in Kundiawa, as George Brixey and Laurie had started the work there. Again, God's work was expanding.

It was time for our second furlough. When we returned to the U.S. in December of 1966, we left behind 166 churches, five school buildings, a large headquarters church, an enlarged first aid station, and a trade store that had now become a general store to serve the natives in that area. We also now had a power plant which furnished electricity from 5:30 p.m. until 10:30 p.m. We had four homes to accommodate our staff of missionaries and teachers. Forty-nine native pastors had received sufficient training to minister to their own people. Some of these could neither read nor write. But they memorized Bible stories and with a picture roll under their arm, they trudged the jungle trails to give the good news of the gospel to those who never yet had heard.

The Mission Board sent Paul and Darlene Palmer and their three sons to fill in for us while we were on furlough. There had already been some discussion about opening a church in Goroka. While we were on furlough, Paul began this process. The Palmers ministered for awhile in Goroka. Then Dean and Nancy Paterson, who had been working with the school and mission in

Hageri, moved to Goroka and ministered in the work there. Also, Roy and Gloria Matthews joined the Foursquare team being sent from the Perth Foursquare churches. They also ministered for awhile at Hageri and then moved to Goroka.

God continued to perform miracles—many healings, witch doctors giving their hearts to Jesus, and by this time we had lost count of how many had been raised from the dead. God was showing these primitive people what a powerful God they had became acquainted with as they exercised their faith in Him.

LAE

While on furlough, Mason talked to Dr. Edwards concerning moving our family to the coastal town of Lae. Many of the Christian nationals had moved to Lae to work, and there was no full gospel church there. This was also the coastal town where all of the cargo arriving for the missionaries was cleared. Another big factor was that Virgene was finding it more difficult to teach four children in addition to all of the responsibilities of the mission. And now Denise, our fifth, was ready to start school. Lae had one of the two high schools in New Guinea for expatriate children in addition to three primary schools. The government was also building the technological branch of the University of PNG in Lae. This would open up another area of ministry. So the Mission Board granted permission for us to move to Lae when we arrived back in January 1968 to begin our next term of service. Again mission leases had to be obtained for our home and church, which came through quickly. And, again God smiled down upon His work.

Mason and Virgene's home in Lae, built by Mason

All the men joined forces to build our house in Lae. God had blessed the mission with builders, electricians, painters, plumbers, etc.—all licensed. The weather was now different; we no longer had the beautiful mountain air but instead had hot tropical heat—day and night, 365 days of the year. The children loved school, and Virgene enjoyed her freedom from teaching so she now could give full time to teaching the women and Sunday school and working in the office assisting Mason with the responsibilities of growing missions.

After we moved to Lae, others continued to join the Foursquare mission. Among them were Barry and Rose Silverback and their four children, who moved to Hageri along with John and Vivian Sweeney, Wayne and Lorraine Bowering, Roy and Gloria Matthews, and Greg and Sue Biddell. Yvonne Wilson returned to Adelaide, married Ian Chamberlin, and they both returned to Hageri to minister. Garth and Mary Van Huet with their two daughters joined the team.

One day Barry Silverback came to Mason saying that he was very busy with mission work but had a real burden to start an English Bible school. Mason gave him his blessing, and it was started in 1968 at Hageri. What a thrill it was for us to attend graduation services at both Bible schools! Now there were three types of indigenous pastors: those who still could not read or write, those who preached in Pidgin, and those who could preach in English.

The work continued to grow and multiply with more pastors and workers. The conventions grew larger to some 4,000–6,000 attendees and were now held at Kapakamarigi. Mason also felt it was time to have an executive council comprised of missionaries and national pastors. This proved to be a great success. Soon there were more nationals than missionaries on the council and the nationals were beginning to plan the conventions and the camps.

Not long after arriving back in New Guinea after our third furlough, Mason received a letter from Dr. Leland Edwards saying that the Mission Board had voted to make him director not only of Foursquare missions in New Guinea but also Australia. This meant his responsibilities became even greater.

During this time others continued to join the Foursquare family. Jeff and Jeanette Driscoll came from Adelaide, and Larry and Joanne Six and their three children came from the U.S. By this time the English Bible school had been taken over by Larry Six. Barry and Rose Silverback had gone on furlough; when they came back they felt burdened for Port Moresby. That was wonderful! Mason contacted the Los Angeles Foursquare Missions Department about it, but they felt they could not finance a new work at that time. So Mason gave the Silverbacks his blessing as they opened the mission work for CRC, which had grown and multiplied tremendously. Meanwhile, the Pidgin Bible school was going wonderfully at Gotomi. Later another couple wrote and said they wanted to join the mission, Jessie and Mary Theoador, also from the Philippines. The work was expanding into the Enga and many other areas.

In 1972 it was time for our fourth furlough. Jeff and Jeanette Driscoll moved down from the Highlands to replace us. Jeff was a very good administrator; and by that time a native pastor, Inagori, was pastoring the growing Lae church. During our furlough the work continued to grow. We were very pleased with how the work had progressed when we returned. Shortly after our return, John Sweeney introduced the Abner family to us. It was always a special pleasure to meet another American family. Harold, Linda, Hal, and Hank were stationed in the Bena Bena with the New Life League Mission organization in 1972. John and Harold would frequently drive to Lae to buy building supplies and visit with us in our Lae home. (Their eldest son, Hal, and our youngest daughter, Denise, grew up together. They were married in Los Angeles, California, in 1987.)

Miss Merrilyn Teague, a missionary from Australia, was asked to assume the position of director of Christian education in New Guinea. In February 1972 a six-week teacher training course in Pidgin was held for fourteen teachers. Eight schools averaging thirty pupils each were open and five more were scheduled to open by the first of 1973. All became self supporting. Missionaries continued to finish their terms. Some returned and some felt they had accomplished their work in New Guinea. Con and Dorothy Vermuelen and their three children from Perth joined the team. Like others, they were a great blessing to the work.

The year of 1975 was a historic marker, as New Guinea

became an independent country and took the combined name of Papua New Guinea. Everyone prayed it would go smoothly; and it did, praise the Lord.

In 1976 Phil and Diane Franklin and their four children joined us in Lae for a period of time. Then they transferred to the Highlands. In 1977 Ken Goodenough joined us working with the church in Lae. One day we received a letter from the Philippines from a young lady, Angelita Lagasca, who had been our secretary when we were in Manila. She told us she had a burden to come to Papua New Guinea and teach in the Bible college. What a thrill it was to have her! She had much knowledge to share, as she had taught in the Philippines. Later Monesto and Jojo Ysugi came to help teach in the English Bible college at Kapakamarigi. Then Jessie and Mary Theoador joined the station. Ruth Pearson had gone to the U.S. and graduated from Mount Vernon Bible College. She married Bruce Redner and returned to minister for a time at Kapakamarigi. Later Merv and Linda McKean moved to Kapakamarigi to do auto maintenance.

In 1977 we received a letter from Dr. Edwards saying that the Mission Board wanted to make a movie on how the Foursquare work began in Papua New Guinea. He said a Christian filming team would be arriving soon to make it. The company was GMT—Great and Mighty Things. Allen Hauge came first to look over the sites and tell us what would have to be done to get ready. In August the team arrived, as it had to be filmed in the dry season. The film *Cargo from the Silver Bird* took three long, hard weeks to film. But what a blessing it has been in many countries! We showed it at the next convention. What an exciting time it was for so many to see themselves on the screen!

During the year of 1978, the Lord began to deal with us that the work He had for us in PNG had been accomplished. At that time nearly every church was being pastored by a national. The Lord told us He had other work for us to do. This was hard for us to hear, as we were so happy in our work and we loved the people of PNG so much. During the annual missionary conference, a word of prophecy was given by the guest speaker—a man who did not even know us. He confirmed that God was speaking to us to leave PNG.

In a few months we reluctantly wrote to Dr. Edwards, telling him and the Mission Board what God was saying to us. Dr. Edwards replied, "We know you are God's children; and that if this is what He is asking you to do, then we will be behind you." They began to look for a replacement for us. On December 1, 1979, Rev. Phil Starr arrived in Lae, soon to be followed by his wife, Millie. The Starrs had been ministering in the Philippines for several years.

Mason spent the next three weeks in orientation with Phil getting him acquainted with the people, pastors, roads, areas, and mission policies. We boarded the plane to leave PNG the third week of December 1979, not knowing what God had next for us to do. But we had no doubt that He knew. Thus we ended twenty-three years in Papua New Guinea, leaving behind 165 churches and some 13,000 converts. To God be the glory!

ABOUT THE AUTHORS

Mason and Virgene Hughes

While attending Life Bible College in Los Angeles, Mason and Virgene married in 1949. They were ordained as Foursquare Ministers in 1952. After serving as pastors in Foursquare churches throughout Ohio and Canada, they were appointed as the first Foursquare gospel missionaries to pioneer a new work in New Guinea. They served there from 1956 to 1979. During those twenty-three years in Papua New Guinea, they witnessed a supernatural move of God. In 1980 the International Church of the Foursquare Gospel bestowed an honorary degree of doctor of divinity on Mason for the outstanding work accomplished in Papua New Guinea.

In 1982 they were appointed as missionaries to Singapore to establish the Foursquare Gospel Church in Southeast Asia. They ministered and encouraged pastors and churches in all of Southeast Asia. Responding to a need for leadership training, they helped established works in Malaysia, Thailand, Indonesia, Burma, Sri Lanka, Pakistan, and Nepal.

Though their fondness for tropical fruit and spicy food exemplify the lingering effects of so many years in Southeast Asia, Mason and Virgene are now thoroughly enjoying many of the things they missed while spending that time on the mission field. They have a home of their own in Concord, North Carolina, where they faithfully serve in the Foursquare church as ministers to the seniors. They are active and present in the lives of their family, excited to be able to perform weddings and celebrate birthdays, anniversaries, and other special times. Virgene enjoys knitting for all fifteen grandchildren and twenty-eight great grandchildren and nurturing the many

African violets that grace their living room. Mason is a master craftsman creating a wide variety of custom leaded and stained glass products. They both enjoy the flora and fauna (especially the many varieties of birds) that thrive in their lovely backyard.

Their interest in and heart for missions has not waned. They have served in several short-term missions assignments and willingly travel and speak on a wide range of missions topics.

Hal and Denise Abner

Hal and Denise grew up together on the mission field in Papua New Guinea. They were married in Los Angeles, California, in 1987. They have two daughters, Natasha and Nicole. The family has continued to be actively involved in missions. Hal and Denise lead short-term mission trips to Central America, the Caribbean, and Africa; lecture on missions at schools and churches; and are consultants to individuals and ministries on foreign mission strategies.

After retiring from a twenty-year Army career, which took the family several places in the world, Hal earned his PhD in leadership and higher education. When he's not sharing about missions, he's teaching karate at The Academy of Christian Martial Arts, in Hampton, Virginia, with his daughter, Natasha, who graduated from Liberty University in 2012 as an RN. Nicole graduated in 2014 from Johnson and Wales University as a pastry chef.

Denise graduated from Christ for the Nations Institute (CFNI) in 1982. She then joined with her parents to pioneer a Foursquare work in Singapore. She returned to school, graduating from LIFE Bible College in 1987. In addition to her duties as a U.S. Army wife and mother of two bright and active girls, Denise served as a religious education coordinator (Korea), volunteered at the Red Cross, and worked as director of missions at

Covenant Love Family Church in Fayetteville, North Carolina. Besides raising their children, Denise has also enjoyed raising two fish, two turtles, four crabs, a ton of rabbits, two ninja hamsters, a possessive Yorkie/Silky Terrier named Joy, a cockatiel named Butterbean, and a spoiled cat that answers to Quinton.

CONTACT THE AUTHORS

You can visit us at
www.5000arrows.com

Write us at
5000pngarrows@gmail.com

MORE BOOKS
TO EDIFY & INSPIRE YOU

CREATION HOUSE HAS BEEN AN INDUSTRY LEADER FOR
MORE THAN 40 YEARS WITH WORLDWIDE DISTRIBUTION AND
A REPUTATION FOR QUALITY AND INTEGRITY.

WAYNE ABEL

978-1-62136-387-3
$10.99 US

A NOVEL OF SUSPENSE

AMY SANDERS

978-1-62136-392-7
$16.99 US

Foreword by Jeb Bush

RANDALL JAMES

978-1-62136-396-5
$16.99 US

STEVE RICHARD

978-1-62136-672-0
$14.99 US

VISIT YOUR LOCAL BOOKSTORE
WWW.CREATIONHOUSE.COM

RETAILERS: CALL 1-800-283-8494
WWW.CHARISMAHOUSEB2B.COM

CREATION
HOUSE

12461